Truffles are in season in the autumn and early winter months, and you can find them in specialist delicatessens. They are very expensive but a great treat. It really isn't worth using truffles from a can or jar as they bear no resemblance to the flavour of fresh truffles.

 An abundance of fresh fish and shellfish is available in Italy. Chargrilling and simple cooking are the most popular methods of treating fresh fish.

Parmesan shavings are best made with a mandoline, but you can also use a vegetable peeler.

30 Minute Italian

30 Minute Italian

Cook modern recipes in 30 minutes or under using Arborio Rice, Polenta, Porcini, Morels, Orzo, Linguine, Fontina, Pecorino, Pancetta, Marsala, Cavolo Nero, Truffle Oil, Pumpkin Seed Oil, Saffron and Balsamic Vinegar.

Fran Warde

Photography by David Loftus

HAMLYN

30 Minute Italian
Fran Warde

First published in 1998 by
Hamlyn, reprinted in 1999
an imprint of Octopus Publishing Group Ltd.
2-4 Heron Quays, Docklands London, E14 4JP.

British Library Cataloguing-in-Publication Data
A catalogue record for this book is available from
the British Library.

ISBN 0 600 59426 2

Main text set in 8½ on 12pt Arial and
Monotype Grotesque Light.

Printed in China

Publishing Director: Laura Bamford
Commissioning Editor: Nicola Hill
Editors: Anne Crane and Katey Day

Art Director: Keith Martin
Executive Art Editor: Mark Stevens
Designer: Peter Gerrish

Photographer: David Loftus
Home Economist: Fran Warde
Stylist: Wei Tang
Indexer: Hilary Bird

Production Controller: Katherine Hockley

Notes
1. All recipes serve 4 unless otherwise stated.
2. Standard level spoon measurements are used in all recipes.
   1 tablespoon = one 15 ml spoon
   1 teaspoon = one 5 ml spoon
3. Both imperial and metric measurements have been given in all recipes. Use one set of measurements only and not a mixture of both.
4. Eggs should be medium (size 3) unless otherwise stated.
5. Milk should be full fat unless otherwise stated.
6. Fresh herbs should be used unless otherwise stated. If unavailable use dried herbs as an alternative but halve the quantities stated.
7. Ovens should be preheated to the specified temperature – if using a fan assisted oven, follow the manufacturer's instructions for adjusting the time and temperature.

Contents

Introduction

Cooking for me started at a very young age when I would help my mum in the kitchen (I'm not sure if it was help but it was always great fun), spilling sugar and flour everywhere and seeing who could mix the fastest! As soon as she taught me that part of cooking was also clearing up, I was allowed to cook more and more: cakes on Saturday afternoon then, later, fish pies and lasagne. I went to a boarding school with dreadful food, but on Tuesdays it was domestic science; I would try to make a decent meal for a few friends to enjoy. Everyone relied on it working out, which it generally did.

I think that these early days played a great part in creating the foundations for my cooking career. I still enjoy it and continue to learn: it's a never-ending creative process of combining colours, flavours and textures to produce a delicious meal to enjoy with friends.

I have aimed to produce imaginative and tasty recipes which are quick and simple to make (and good for you, too). The recipes in this book have been designed to show that it is possible to produce delicious, mouthwatering meals in 30 minutes – the same length of time that it takes to heat up many ready-made meals – or even less time, without resorting to convenience food.

Italian recipes fit the bill perfectly when you need good quick meals in a hurry for the Italians are very keen on fresh food and speedy methods of preparation. They take their food very seriously, combining a deep respect for top-quality ingredients with a great love of home cooking – in fact the way to enjoy Italian food at its best is to eat in people's homes.

Italian food, in all its rich, regional diversity, doesn't just taste delicious, it's actually good for you too. The Mediterranean diet, with its emphasis on fresh vegetables and fruit, fresh fish and seafood, pasta and olive oil, is reckoned to be one of the healthiest in the world, full of vitamins and minerals and low in saturated fat.

In this book I have included a lot of vegetables which work very well as supper dishes on their own. Serve two or three vegetable, pasta or rice dishes together, enjoy their delicate flavours, and see how satisfied you feel after the meal without feeling at all heavy or as if you have eaten too much. There are some delicious meat and fish recipes, too, which can be cooked in 30 minutes, a joy

to any busy cook who doesn't want to be chained to the stove when the sun is shining outside or after a busy day at work or with the children. There are also some puddings for special days. I have to say that I am especially proud of the chocolate risotto, which is a totally new idea and is easy to make from ingredients which will be found in any well-stocked kitchen.

Do follow the Italian example and shop carefully, though. Some of the cheaper products in our shops and supermarkets are very poor substitutes for the real thing. Never, for example, buy ready-grated Parmesan, instead buy a piece and grate it as required. A guide to the most important or unusual ingredients used in the recipes appears in the glossary that follows.

Ivan Warde.

Glossary

Balsamic vinegar
This aristocrat of vinegars is made in Modena. The grape juice is aged in wooden barrels for an average of seven years. Like a good wine, it needs time to mature, and the longer it is in the barrel the deeper and sweeter the flavour – and the higher the price.

Capers
Used to flavour sauces, these are the pungent, sharp-tasting buds of a shrub found in Mediterranean countries. Capers are usually bottled in brine and need to be rinsed in water before using. Small ones are the best.

Cavolo nero
A long, slim cabbage with a distinct sweet flavour; it is a beautiful green with a hint of purplish black.

Chocolate
Bars of chocolate vary so much in their cocoa content. Look on the back of the packet and only use ones which contain at least 70% cocoa solids. I prefer Valrhona which can be found in good delicatessens.

Cheeses
Dolcelatte A soft creamy cows' milk cheese with blue veins, aged for 2 months; it is similar to Gorgonzola but milder.
Fontina A soft cows' milk cheese from the Val d'Aosta in the Italian Alps, which is aged for up to five months. It is reminiscent of Gruyère and used in cooking and as a dessert cheese.
Mascarpone A soft creamy cheese made with cows' milk and used for sweet and savoury dishes.
Mozzarella Originally made from buffalos' milk, it is now more often made from cows' milk or a mixture of the two. Cows' milk mozzarella does not have the same softness of flavour. Mozzarella should be eaten fresh; it melts well and is frequently used on pizzas.
Parmesan This strong, hard cheese is made from partially skimmed cows' milk and aged for up to two years. The best Parmesan has the words *Parmigiano-Reggiano* punched in to the rind. Buy it in a block and grate it as you need it.
Pecorino This ewes' milk cheese can be soft or hard depending on its age; it is made all over Italy so flavours can vary greatly. Mature, hard pecorino is used for grating like Parmesan.
Ricotta A bland, soft, fresh cheese used as a base in fillings and frequently combined with spinach. It should be used when it is very fresh.

Ciabatta
A popular Italian bread baked in to a flat loaf with a distinctive open texture. It can have a range of flavourings added.

Fennel
A beautiful fragrant vegetable with a delicate aniseed flavour, fennel is wonderful with fish; use the feathery fronds to add to salsa verde.

Focaccia
A flat yeast bread made with olive oil and baked in an oiled pan. It is often flavoured with garlic, herbs, sun-dried tomatoes or olives.

Garlic A pungent herb used extensively in Italian cooking. Crush heavily with the side of a knife to remove the papery skin, then the clove can be chopped.

Herbs

Basil The best-known Italian herb with soft, bright green leaves, basil is a vital ingredient in pesto and goes well with tomatoes. There is also a red basil with small, purplish leaves and a more delicate flavour.
Bay leaves Usually used dried in soups and stews as part of a bouquet garni.
Oregano A sweet, spicy and aromatic herb, similar to marjoram.
Rosemary Its long, spiky leaves give rosemary a distinctive appearance. It is used a great deal in Italy, particularly with chicken and lamb. It is very pungent, so should be used in moderation.

Olive oil Extra virgin olive oil, virgin olive oil and olive oil. These names refer to the way that the oil is extracted and this can greatly alter the flavour. Try to buy extra virgin oil from the first cold pressing as this will be rich in flavour and is most suitable for dressings, sauces and pouring over pasta. A less expensive oil can be used for frying.

Olives Small, oval tree fruits which ripen from green to black. For the best flavour, buy them from delicatessens that sell them loose rather than in bottles or cans.

Pancetta The same cut as streaky bacon but differently cured, pancetta is found in supermarkets or in delicatessens. It is also sold as pancetta arrotolata, in a roll like salami. Buy a 1 cm/½ inch slice, unroll it and use as pancetta.

Panettone A baked yeast cake from Milan enriched with egg yolks, raisins and candied peel. Panettone is traditionally served at Christmas or with coffee; it is very good toasted at breakfast.

Parma ham A great Italian delicacy, this cured ham comes from the area around Parma in the Emilia-Romagna region of northern Italy. The skin is rubbed in salt then the hams are hung in cellars to mature for 8–10 months. Parma ham must be served thinly sliced; it is eaten on its own or with melon or figs.

Pasta This is made from hard durum wheat flour and water. If it is made with eggs, it is called pasta all'ouvo. I prefer fresh pasta but a good dried Italian brand can be substituted. The Italians do not usually eat pasta as a main course, but serve a light pasta dish between the antipasti and the main course. It is available in a bewildering range of shapes and sizes.

Pasta shapes

Farfalle or farfallini Pasta bows.
Fusilli Pasta twists or corkscrews.
Lasagne Large sheets of pasta used for baked dishes. Sheets can be cut to fit cooking dishes.
Linguine Long, thin, flat ribbon noodles.
Pappardelle Wide pasta noodles.
Penne Sometimes known as quills, these are a short, tubular lengths of pasta.
Orecchiette Small, round ear-shaped pasta.
Orzo A very small pasta shape, which looks rather like grains of rice.
Spaghetti Long, string-like pasta.
Tagliatelle Long, flat ribbon noodles.
Tortellini Pasta twists with various fillings.

Pine nuts Small, slim, soft nuts with an oily texture, these come from the Mediterranean stone pine tree. Pine nuts, also known as pine kernels, are used in pasta sauces, stuffings and salads and are usually browned before using. They turn rancid quickly so store them in a refrigerator.

Polenta Ground maize (corn) kernels mixed with water, made in to a flat golden loaf, sliced and grilled. Polenta needs to be flavoured as it is bland, although it is rich in vitamins. It can also be served in a softer form, like mashed potatoes.

Pumpkin seed oil Pressed from roasted pumpkin seeds, this thick, brown oil, tinged with green, has a powerful, toasted flavour.

Puy lentils Small, round lentils, greenish brown in colour and far superior to any other lentil for texture and flavour. They come from the area around Le Puy in France.

Risotto rice Arborio is the classic risotto rice from Piedmont. It absorbs a lot of cooking liquid without becoming too soft. The grain is plump and irregular, translucent at the edges with a hard, white core. It produces a creamy risotto with a slight bite. Carnaroli is very similar.

Saffron The dried stigmas of a species of crocus, with a pungent aroma, bitter flavour and a beautiful golden colour. Buy it in Spain or at duty-free shops where it is cheaper and comes in larger containers.

Sea salt I think Maldon sea salt from Essex is by far the best; there are no additives and the large flaky crystals are fantastic on a salad or used at the table.

Squashes These are members of the marrow and pumpkin family; the best is butternut squash for its sweet flavour and dense texture.

Sun-dried tomatoes Intensely flavoured dried tomatoes which add zip to a dish. Those bottled in oil are more convenient to use than the dried variety, which need to be soaked before use.

Truffle oil The infusion of truffle juices in to an oil, usually extra virgin olive oil. White truffle oil is usually more expensive and stronger in flavour than black truffle oil. Use both sparingly as they have an intense flavour.

Wild mushrooms

Chanterelles Wonderful aromatic mushrooms with a perfumed taste, chanterelles are shaped like open horns, torn around the edges. They vary in colour from brown to gold and dry well.
Morels Mushrooms with bulbous pitted caps and an intense aroma. Fresh morels need to be cleaned well. They are also found dried and bottled.
Porcini Delicious mushrooms with a deep, rich flavour, porcini have a round, bun-like cap, a thick chubby stalk and fleshy texture. They are sold fresh and dried. Soak dried porcini in hot water for 15 minutes before use, then drain, filter and reserve the water to use as a rich stock.
Truffles The mysterious king of fungi, these are found below ground near oak trees and are sniffed out by pigs or dogs in autumn and winter. Usually the size of a walnut, truffles are rough on the outside, dense inside and firm to the touch. Both white and black truffles are found; their flavour is so intense that only a little is needed. Truffles are best served raw, finely shaved over salad or pasta.

Soups

In Italy soup is served as a *primo piatto*, first course, as an alternative to rice or pasta. Many of the soups are hearty, based on beans, vegetables and bread and thus make complete meals in themselves.

Preparation time **10 minutes**　Cooking time **20 minutes**
Total time **30 minutes**　*Serves 4*

spinach and broccoli soup

one　Heat the oil and butter in a saucepan, add the onion and garlic and sauté for 3 minutes.

two　Add the chopped potatoes, broccoli, spinach and stock, bring to the boil and simmer for 15 minutes.

three　This soup can be liquidized or left with chunky pieces. Add the Gorgonzola to the soup with the lemon juice, nutmeg and salt and pepper to taste. Garnish with the toasted pine nuts and serve with warm crusty bread.

2 tablespoons olive oil
50 g/2 oz butter
1 onion, diced
1 garlic clove, crushed and chopped
2 potatoes, chopped
250 g/8 oz broccoli, chopped
300 g/10 oz spinach, washed and chopped
900 ml/1½ pints chicken or vegetable stock
125 g/4 oz Gorgonzola cheese, crumbled in to small pieces
juice of ½ lemon
½ teaspoon grated nutmeg
salt and pepper
75 g/3 oz toasted pine nuts, to garnish

Preparation time **10 minutes**　Total time **10 minutes**　*Serves 4*

melon and Parma ham soup

1 ripe cantaloupe or charentais melon, weighing about 1.5 kg/3 lb
8 slices Parma ham
salt and pepper
red basil leaves, to garnish

one　Cut the melon in half and remove the seeds. Scoop the flesh in to a food processor and whizz until smooth, then add salt and pepper to taste.

two　Finely dice 4 of the ham slices and stir them in to the soup. Cut the remaining 4 slices in to thin ribbons.

three　Garnish the soup with the ham ribbons and torn basil leaves.

Serve at room temperature or just slightly chilled.
When food is too cold you cannot taste its full flavour.

Preparation time **10 minutes**
Cooking time **20 minutes**
Total time **30 minutes**   *Serves 4*

pesto and green vegetable soup

Pesto:
3 garlic cloves, crushed and chopped
handful of basil leaves
2 tablespoons pine nuts
50 g/2 oz Parmesan cheese, freshly grated
3 tablespoons olive oil
Soup:
3 tablespoons olive oil
1 onion, diced
2 leeks, sliced
1 potato, chopped
425 g/14 oz can haricot beans, drained and rinsed
1.5 litres/2½ pints vegetable stock
2 courgettes, diced
125 g/4 oz small green beans, cut in to small pieces
125 g/4 oz broccoli florets, chopped
250 g/8 oz canned artichoke hearts
1 tablespoon flat leaf parsley, chopped
salt and pepper

one   To make the pesto, put the garlic, basil, pine nuts and Parmesan in a food processor or blender and purée thoroughly. Add the oil and blend again. Set aside.

two   Heat the oil for the soup in a saucepan, add the onion and leeks and cook over a gentle heat for about 3 minutes.

three Add the potato, haricot beans, stock and salt and pepper to taste, bring to the boil and simmer for 12 minutes.

four   Add the courgettes, green beans, broccoli and artichoke hearts and simmer for 5 minutes.

five   Finally, add the chopped parsley and pesto and stir well. Serve immediately with warm focaccia bread.

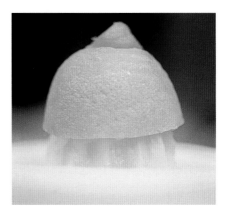

Preparation time **5 minutes**
Cooking time **25 minutes**
Total time **30 minutes**
Serves 4

courgette soup

This soup is delicious served cold in the summer, as the lemon gives it a really fresh clean taste.

2 tablespoons olive oil
4 shallots, diced
1 garlic clove, crushed and chopped
6 courgettes, diced
2 potatoes, chopped
1.2 litres/2 pints chicken stock
75 g/3 oz farfallini or other small pasta
juice and rind of 1 lemon
large handful of chives, chopped
salt and pepper

one   Heat the oil in a saucepan, add the shallots and garlic and sauté gently for 3 minutes.

two   Add the courgettes, potatoes and stock, simmer for 15 minutes, then pass through a sieve or liquidize until smooth.

three Add the pasta and cook for about 7 minutes until soft.

four   Stir in the lemon rind, juice and chives. Season with salt and pepper and serve at once.

Preparation time **5 minutes**   Cooking time **25 minutes**   Total time **30 minutes**   *Serves 4*

butternut squash soup

1 butternut squash, weighing 875 g/1¾ lb
50 g/2 oz butter
2 tablespoons olive oil
2 onions, chopped
1 garlic clove, crushed and chopped
1 litre/1¾ pints chicken or vegetable stock
pinch of saffron threads
salt and pepper
To serve:
2 rosemary sprigs, chopped
75 g/3 oz Parmesan cheese, freshly grated

one   To prepare the squash, cut it in half and remove all the seeds, peel off the skin and chop the flesh in to small dice.

two   Heat the butter and oil in a saucepan, add the onion, garlic and squash and sauté for 5 minutes.

three   Add the stock and saffron, bring to the boil and simmer for 15 minutes.

four   Pour the soup in to a food processor and work to a purée. Season generously with salt and pepper.

five   To serve, ladle in to warmed bowls and sprinkle each one with chopped rosemary and a generous spoonful of grated Parmesan.

Preparation time **5 minutes**
Cooking time **25 minutes**
Total time **30 minutes**   *Serves 4*

minestrone soup

Minestrone improves when it is made in advance and reheated. Cover and store in the refrigerator so that the flavours can blend.

2 tablespoons olive oil
1 onion, diced
1 garlic clove, crushed and chopped
2 celery sticks, chopped
1 leek, finely sliced
1 carrot, chopped
400 g/13 oz can chopped tomatoes
600 ml/1 pint chicken or vegetable stock
1 courgette, diced
½ small cabbage, shredded
1 bay leaf
75 g/3 oz canned haricot beans
75 g/3 oz spaghetti, broken in to small pieces
1 tablespoon chopped flat leaf parsley
salt and pepper
To serve:
50 g/2 oz Parmesan cheese, freshly grated
Bruschetta (see page 20)

one   Heat the oil in a saucepan, add the onion, garlic, celery, leek and carrot and sauté for 3 minutes.

two   Add the tomatoes, stock, courgette, cabbage, bay leaf and haricot beans. Bring to the boil and simmer for 10 minutes.

three   Add the broken spaghetti and season with salt and pepper to taste. Stir well and cook for a further 8 minutes. Keep stirring as the soup may stick to the bottom of the pan.

four   Just before serving add the chopped parsley and stir well. Serve with grated Parmesan and bruschetta.

Like Minestrone, Tuscan bean soup can be reheated and, as it improves with keeping, it is really worth making the day before and storing in the refrigerator, allowing all the flavours to mingle.

Preparation time **5 minutes**   Cooking time **25 minutes**   Total time **30 minutes**   *Serves 4*

Tuscan bean soup

2 tablespoons olive oil
4 shallots, chopped
2 garlic cloves, crushed and chopped
150 g/5 oz piece of green bacon, diced
1 carrot, diced
2 celery sticks, diced
½ red pepper, cored, deseeded and diced
425 g/14 oz can borlotti beans, drained and rinsed
1 litre/1¾ pints chicken stock
1 bay leaf
1 teaspoon chopped oregano
1 teaspoon chopped marjoram
handful of flat leaf parsley, chopped
salt and pepper
extra virgin olive oil, to drizzle

one   Heat the oil in a saucepan, add the shallots, garlic, bacon, carrot, celery and red pepper and cook, stirring occasionally, for 5 minutes.

two   Add the beans, stock, bay leaf, oregano and marjoram, bring to the boil and simmer for 15 minutes. Skim off any scum that may come from the beans.

three   Taste and season well. Finally, just before serving, add the chopped parsley.

four   To serve, ladle in to warmed bowls and drizzle each one with a little extra virgin olive oil.

Preparation time **10 minutes**   Cooking time **10 minutes**   Total time **20 minutes**   *Serves 4*

mussel soup

one   Warm the olive oil in a large saucepan. Add the onions, garlic, chilli and bacon and sauté for 5 minutes.

two   Check the mussels carefully. Discard any which are open or do not close immediately when tapped on a work surface.

three   Add the mussels, tomatoes, wine, saffron and season with salt and pepper; mix well. Place a tight-fitting lid on the pan and simmer for 5 minutes, or until all the mussel shells have opened. Discard any mussels with shells which remain shut.

four   Add the parsley, stir well and serve at once.

2 tablespoons olive oil
2 onions, chopped
2 garlic cloves, crushed and chopped
1 red chilli, chopped
150 g/5 oz piece of green bacon, chopped
1 kg/2 lb mussels, scrubbed and debearded
2 x 400 g/13 oz cans chopped tomatoes
½ bottle dry white wine
good pinch of saffron threads
handful of flat leaf parsley, roughly chopped
salt and pepper

Preparation time **5 minutes**   Cooking time **5 minutes**
Total time **10 minutes**   *Serves 4*

bruschetta

8 slices ciabatta bread
2 garlic cloves, peeled
small handful of flat leaf parsley, chopped
5 tablespoons olive oil
salt

Bruschetta is delicious served with many different Italian dishes, especially soup and fish. It is a very useful accompaniment as the bread does not have to be fresh.

one   Toast the bread under a preheated grill until golden brown.

two   Rub the garlic over one side of the bread; the bread acts as a grater and the garlic is evenly spread over the bread. Sprinkle the bruschetta with the parsley and salt and drizzle with olive oil. Serve immediately or keep warm until required but do not keep warm for too long or the bruschetta will lose its crunchiness.

Preparation time **10 minutes**
Cooking time **5 minutes**
Total time **15 minutes**
Serves 4

crostini

8 slices ciabatta bread
2 garlic cloves, peeled
small handful of flat leaf parsley, chopped
5 tablespoons olive oil
1–2 red peppers, peeled and sliced in to strips
75 g/3 oz black olives, pitted
125 g/4 oz goats' cheese, crumbled
salt and pepper

one   Toast the bread under a preheated grill until golden brown.

two   Rub the garlic over the bread on one side; the bread acts as a grater and the garlic is evenly spread over the bread. Sprinkle with parsley and salt and drizzle with olive oil.

three   Mix together the red peppers, olives and crumbled goats' cheese and season with pepper.

four   Spread the mixture evenly over the toasted bruschetta and place under a preheated low grill for 2 minutes to just melt the cheese. Serve at once.

Variation: Sliced tomatoes, sprinkled with oregano and pepper, are also very good on bruschetta.

Crostini are an extension of bruschetta, the base is
the same but the crostini have many different
toppings. They are great with soup; if you want to
serve a simple supper there is nothing better than
a good home-made soup, crostini with your
favourite topping and a fresh green salad.

Pasta

Well over 200 different shapes of pasta are available in Italy and every region has its own particular specialities and ways of serving them. Pasta is one of the most versatile Italian foods and may be baked, stuffed and tossed in sauces or dressings.

Preparation time **10 minutes**   Cooking time **10 minutes**   Total time **20 minutes**   *Serves 4*

linguine with vegetables

1 red pepper, cored, deseeded
and cut in to large squares
1 courgette, sliced
1 red onion, sliced
1 small aubergine, sliced in to
thin rounds
8 asparagus spears, trimmed
5 tablespoons olive oil
300 g/10 oz linguine
3 tablespoons frozen petits pois
125 g/4 oz Parmesan cheese,
freshly grated
handful of basil leaves,
roughly torn
salt and pepper

one   The vegetables can be cooked either on a griddle or grilled. To griddle them, heat the griddle pan then add the peppers, skin side down, and griddle until the skin blisters and blackens. Griddle the courgette, onion and aubergine slices and the asparagus for 2 minutes on each side. Alternatively, cook all the vegetables under a preheated hot grill.

two   Place a large saucepan of water on to boil for the pasta.

three Peel the skin off the pepper and slice in to ribbons. Place in a dish with the courgettes, onion, aubergine and asparagus, drizzle with olive oil and put in to a warm oven to keep warm.

four   Place the pasta in the boiling water and cook for 3–4 minutes if fresh and 8 minutes if dried, or according to packet instructions. Test a piece before draining. Add the petits pois for the last minute of the cooking time.

five   Drain the pasta and petits pois in a colander then return to the saucepan. Add the warm vegetables, season with salt and pepper and add the Parmesan. Toss well, using two spoons, adding a little more olive oil if necessary. Finally add the torn basil leaves and toss again, then serve immediately.

Preparation time **15 minutes**   Cooking time **15 minutes**
Total time **30 minutes**   *Serves 4*

pasta primavera

2 tablespoons olive oil
1 garlic clove, crushed and chopped
2 shallots, chopped
125 g/4 oz shelled peas
125 g/4 oz young broad beans, shelled and grey
skins removed
125 g/4 oz asparagus, trimmed and cut in to
lengths
125 g/4 oz spinach, washed and chopped
300 g/10 oz tagliatelle
150 ml/¼ pint whipping cream
75 g/3 oz Parmesan cheese,
freshly grated
handful of mint leaves, chopped
salt and pepper

one   Place a large saucepan of water on to boil for the tagliatelle.

two   Heat the oil in a saucepan, add the garlic and shallots and sauté for 3 minutes. Add the peas, broad beans, asparagus and spinach to the shallot mixture. Stir well and cook for 2 minutes.

three Put the tagliatelle in to the boiling water and cook for 3 minutes if fresh and 7 minutes if dried, or according to packet instructions. Stir the pasta while it is cooking.

four   Stir the cream in to the vegetables, mix well and simmer for 3 minutes.

five   Drain the tagliatelle thoroughly, then add the pasta to the vegetable sauce and season well with salt and pepper. Add the Parmesan and mint and toss thoroughly with two spoons. Serve at once.

Cook the vegetables for this dish on a heated griddle pan or under a preheated hot grill; this intensifies the flavours of the vegetables.

Preparation time **5 minutes**   Cooking time **10 minutes**
Total time **15 minutes**   *Serves 4*

saffron bows

300 g/10 oz farfalle
25 g/1 oz butter
150 ml/¼ pint double cream
½ teaspoon saffron threads
salt and pepper
75 g/3 oz Parmesan cheese,
freshly grated, to serve

one   Place a large saucepan of water on to boil for the pasta. When it is boiling, add the pasta and stir well. Cook for 3 minutes if fresh and 6 minutes if dried, or according to packet instructions.

two   Heat the butter and cream in a small saucepan, add the saffron and gently bring to the simmer; the yellow of the saffron will explode in to the cream and a fantastic subtle aroma will fill the kitchen.

three   Drain the pasta well, place in a warmed serving bowl and pour over the saffron sauce. Season with salt and pepper and mix well.

four   Serve the Parmesan at the table and sprinkle just a little over each portion.

Saffron threads are the dried stigmas of a species of crocus. Saffron is a costly spice, but a little is all you need to transform a dish.

Preparation time **10 minutes**
Cooking time **20 minutes**
Total time **30 minutes**
Serves 4

penne with tomato and chilli

one   Heat the oil in a saucepan, add the onion and garlic and sauté until soft, do not let them brown. Add the chillies.

two   Place a large saucepan of water on to boil for the penne. When the water is boiling, add the penne and cook for 6 minutes if fresh and 10 minutes if dried, or according to packet instructions.

three   Cut a cross at the stem end of each tomato. Place the tomatoes in a bowl and pour over boiling water to cover. Leave for 1–2 minutes, then drain and peel off the skins. Cut the tomatoes in to quarters, remove the seeds and cut lengthways in to strips.

four   Add the tomatoes to the onion mixture. Over a low heat, add the sugar, vinegar and salt and pepper. Mix gently and simmer slowly until the pasta is cooked.

five   Drain the pasta well. Stir the parsley in to the tomato sauce. Add the sauce to the pasta, mix well, adding a dash of extra virgin olive oil, if wished. Serve with a bowl of grated Parmesan.

3 tablespoons olive oil
1 onion, chopped
2 garlic cloves, crushed and
    chopped
2 pinches crushed dried chillies,
    or to taste
300 g/10 oz penne
10 plum tomatoes
1 teaspoon sugar
1 teaspoon vinegar
handful of flat leaf parsley, chopped
extra virgin olive oil, optional
salt and pepper
75 g/3 oz Parmesan cheese, freshly
    grated, to serve

Preparation time **5 minutes**   Cooking time **15 minutes**   Total time **20 minutes**   *Serves 4*

fusilli with Parmesan and pine nuts

300 g/10 oz fusilli
125 g/4 oz pine nuts
75 g/3 oz butter
2 tablespoons olive oil
75 g/3 oz Parmesan cheese,
freshly grated
handful of basil leaves
salt and pepper

one   Place a large saucepan of water on to boil for the pasta. Put the fusilli in to the boiling water and cook for 3–4 minutes if fresh, for 7 minutes if dried, or according to packet instructions. Test before draining.

two   Toast the pine nuts under the grill or in a pan over a moderate heat. Watch them all the time and move them around to brown evenly.

three   Melt the butter with the oil in a small saucepan. Drain the pasta well, pour over the butter, season with salt and pepper and toss well.

four   Turn in to a warmed serving dish, sprinkle with the pine nuts, Parmesan and basil leaves and serve immediately.

Preparation time **10 minutes**
Cooking time **15 minutes**
Total time **25 minutes**   *Serves 4*

pappardelle with olives and capers

125 g/4 oz black or green olives, pitted
2 pinches crushed dried chillies
2 tablespoons capers, chopped
7 anchovy fillets, drained and chopped
4 large pieces sun-dried tomatoes soaked in olive oil
300 g/10 oz pappardelle
large handful of parsley, chopped
75 g/3 oz Parmesan cheese, freshly grated
salt and pepper

one   Place a large saucepan of water on to boil for the pappardelle.

two   Roughly chop the olives. Put them in to a saucepan with the chillies, capers and anchovies. Chop the sun-dried tomatoes roughly and add them to the saucepan with 4 tablespoons of the olive oil.

three   Put the pasta in to the boiling water and cook for 4 minutes if fresh and 7 minutes if dried, or according to packet instructions. Test a piece before draining.

four   Gently heat the olive mixture for 4 minutes until warm; do not let it fry.

five   Drain the pasta, add the warmed olive mixture, parsley and Parmesan. Season with salt and pepper. Mix well with two spoons and serve. This dish can also be left to stand for a while and served at room temperature.

Preparation time **5 minutes**
Cooking time **10 minutes**
Total time **15 minutes**   *Serves 4*

spinach tortellini with blue cheese dressing

500 g/1 lb spinach tortellini
300 g/10 oz Gorgonzola or dolcelatte cheese
75 g/3 oz butter
150 ml/¼ pint double cream
pepper

one   Place a large saucepan of water on to boil for the tortellini. Put the pasta in to the boiling water and cook for 5 minutes if fresh and 8–9 if dried, or according to packet instructions. Remove a piece and test, before draining.

two   Crumble the cheese in to a small saucepan, add the butter and cream and place over a low heat to melt the cheese and warm the mixture.

three   Drain the pasta well, add the warm cheese sauce, toss well and serve immediately. This is delicious and very rich; a crisp lightly dressed salad is a good accompaniment.

Preparation time **10 minutes**
Cooking time **10 minutes**
Total time **20 minutes**   *Serves 4*

lemon and basil orzo

one   Place a large saucepan of water on to boil for the orzo.

two   Using a pestle and mortar or a food processor, blend the garlic, basil, olive oil, lemon rind and juice until smooth.

three   Place the orzo in the boiling water and cook for 6–8 minutes, or according to packet instructions.

four   Add the Parmesan to the basil mixture, blend well and season with salt and pepper.

five   Drain the orzo thoroughly. Add the pesto and mix well so that the sauce is distributed evenly throughout the orzo. Serve immediately.

2 garlic cloves, crushed and chopped
large handful of basil leaves
5 tablespoons olive oil
rind and juice of 2 lemons
300 g/10 oz dried orzo
150 g/5 oz Parmesan cheese, freshly grated
salt and pepper

Preparation time **10 minutes**   Cooking time **18 minutes**   Total time **28 minutes**   *Serves 4*

penne with broad beans, asparagus and mint

500 g/1 lb asparagus, trimmed and cut in to 5 cm/2 inch lengths
4 tablespoons olive oil
250 g/8 oz broad beans or peas
300 g/10 oz penne
75 ml/3 fl oz double cream
75 g/3 oz Parmesan cheese, freshly grated
4 tablespoons chopped mint
salt and pepper

one   Place a large saucepan of water on to boil for the pasta.

two   Place the asparagus on a baking sheet, brush generously with olive oil and season with salt and pepper. Place under a preheated grill and cook for 8 minutes, turning as they brown.

three   Meanwhile, cook the broad beans or peas in lightly salted boiling water for 2 minutes.

four   Put the pasta in the boiling water and cook for 6 minutes if fresh and 10 minutes if dried, or according to packet instructions. Remove a piece and test before draining.

five   Pour the cream in to the empty pasta pan over the heat, add the cooked broad beans or peas, grilled asparagus, Parmesan and season with salt and pepper. Return the pasta to the pan, add the mint and toss well with two wooden spoons. Serve at once.

This dish is delicious and very good in the summer because of the fresh taste of the lemon and basil. If orzo is not available, another pasta shape can be substituted.

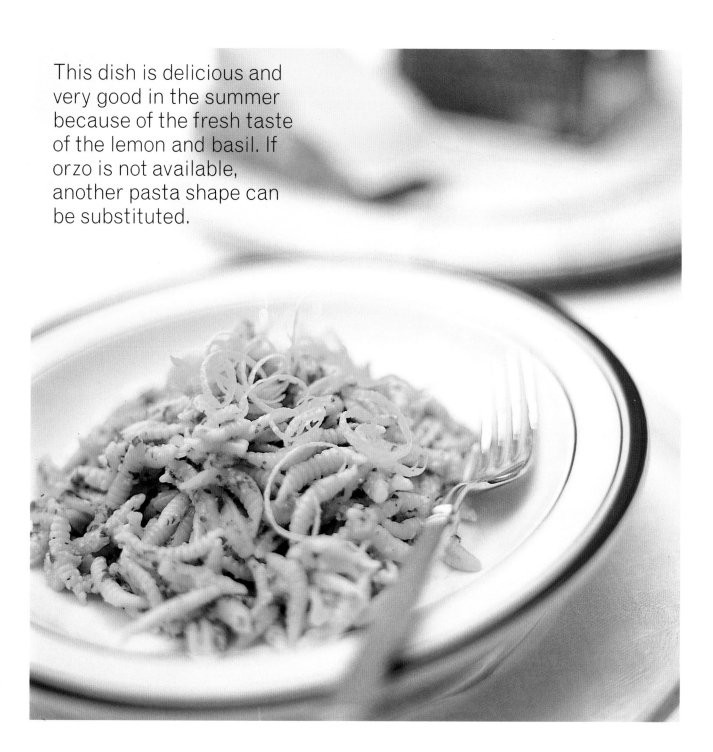

Preparation time **10 minutes**   Cooking time **20 minutes**   Total time **30 minutes**   *Serves 4*

mushroom and mozzarella lasagne stacks

2 tablespoons olive oil
50 g/2 oz butter
2 onions, chopped
2 garlic cloves, crushed and chopped
500 g/1 lb mushrooms, sliced
4 tablespoons double cream
4 tablespoons dry white wine
1 teaspoon chopped thyme
8 pieces fresh lasagne
2 red peppers, cored, deseeded, skinned and thickly sliced
125 g/4 oz packet buffalo mozzarella cheese, sliced
125 g/4 oz baby spinach leaves, washed and trimmed
50 g/2 oz Parmesan cheese
salt and pepper

one   Heat the oil and butter in a saucepan, add the onions and sauté for 3 minutes. Add the garlic and cook for 1 minute.

two   Add the mushrooms, turn up the heat and cook for 5 minutes.

three Add the cream, white wine and thyme, season with salt and pepper and simmer for 4 minutes.

four   Bring a pan of water to the boil, add the lasagne, a few pieces at a time, checking that it does not stick together, and cook for 3 minutes if fresh or 7 minutes if dried. Remove from the pan and place 4 pieces in a well-oiled large ovenproof dish.

five   Place a generous spoonful of mushroom mixture on each piece of lasagne, add some red pepper slices and half of the spinach leaves and put another piece of lasagne on top. Then add the remaining spinach leaves, a slice of mozzarella, and top with a little more mushroom mixture. Finish with some Parmesan shavings. Place the lasagne portions under a preheated very hot grill and cook for 5 minutes until the mushroom mixture is bubbling and the Parmesan is golden.

Preparation time **10 minutes**   Cooking time **10 minutes**
Total time **20 minutes**   *Serves 4*

tagliatelle with fresh truffles

Truffles are in season in the autumn and early winter months, and you can find them in specialist delicatessens. They are very expensive but a great treat. It really isn't worth using truffles from a can or jar as they bear no resemblance to the flavour of fresh truffles.

300 g/10 oz dried tagliatelle
125 g/4 oz truffles
125 g/4 oz butter
½ tablespoon truffle oil
handful of flat leaf parsley, chopped
75 g/3 oz Parmesan cheese, freshly grated
salt and pepper

one   Place a large saucepan of water on to boil for the tagliatelle. Put the pasta in to the boiling water and cook for 8 minutes, or according to packet instructions, stirring from time to time.

two   While the pasta is cooking, clean the truffles with a clean dry soft brush, dusting away any dirt. Finely slice the truffles using a mandoline.

three Drain the pasta, add the butter, truffle oil, parsley, Parmesan and season with salt and pepper to taste and toss well.

four   Add half of the sliced truffles to the pasta and toss again. Serve garnished with the remaining truffles.

This dish can be cooked in advance
except for the final browning of the
Parmesan. Reheat in a moderate oven for
20 minutes, then grill until golden.

Preparation time **10 minutes**   Cooking time **20 minutes**   Total time **30 minutes**   *Serves 4*

spaghetti vongole with flat leaf parsley

1.5 kg/3 lb baby clams (vongole)
4 tablespoons olive oil
2 garlic cloves, crushed and chopped
125 ml/4 fl oz dry white wine
75 ml/3 fl oz double cream
500 g/1 lb spaghetti
large handful of flat leaf parsley, chopped
salt and pepper
freshly grated Parmesan cheese, to serve

one   To wash the vongole, place them in a colander and submerge in a bowl of cold water. Shake vigorously, then lift out the colander and replace with fresh water. Repeat until the vongole are clean, then drain well. Check the vongole and discard any that are damaged or open.

two   Heat the oil in a large saucepan over a low heat, add the garlic and vongole, cover and cook for 3 minutes or until all the vongole have opened. Discard any which do not open.

three   Lift the vongole out of the pan with a slotted spoon. Remove half of them from their shells and return any liquid to the pan. Set the vongole aside.

four   Add the wine and cream to the pan and increase the heat to reduce the sauce.

five   Meanwhile, bring a large pan of boiling water to the boil, add the spaghetti and cook for 3–4 minutes if fresh, 8 minutes if dried, or according to packet instructions, until just tender. Check a piece before draining.

six   Return the vongole to the sauce, stir well, and simmer for 2 minutes. Add the parsley and spaghetti to the vongole, season with salt and pepper and mix well, using two spoons to combine the spaghetti with the sauce.

seven   Serve immediately with freshly grated Parmesan.

Preparation time **5 minutes**   Cooking time **15 minutes**
Total time **20 minutes**   *Serves 4*

tagliatelle with crab sauce

one   Heat the olive oil in a saucepan, add the shallots and sauté gently until soft, but do not brown.

two   Add the crab meat, chillies, lemon rind and juice and season with salt and pepper.

three   Place a large saucepan of water on to boil for the tagliatelle. When it is boiling, add the tagliatelle and cook for 3–4 minutes if fresh, 6 minutes if dried, or according to packet instructions. Test a piece before draining.

four   Add the cream to the crab mixture and bring to the boil.

five   Drain the tagliatelle well. Add the chives to the crab mixture.

six   Add the sauce to the tagliatelle; mix well and serve with a bowl of grated Parmesan.

2 tablespoons olive oil
2 shallots, chopped
200 g/7 oz crab meat
1–2 pinches dried chilli, crumbled
grated rind and juice of 1 lemon
300 g/10 oz tagliatelle
4 tablespoons double cream
handful of chives, snipped
salt and pepper
75 g/3 oz Parmesan cheese, freshly grated, to serve

spaghetti with lobster

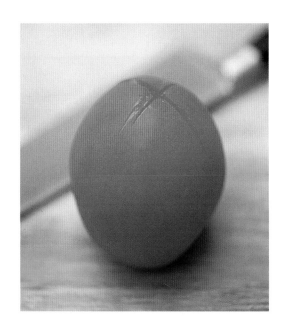

1 kg/2 lb cooked lobster, cut in half lengthways
4 tablespoons olive oil
2 shallots, chopped
8 plum tomatoes, skinned, deseeded and chopped
juice of 1 lemon
300 g/10 oz spaghetti
handful of chives, chopped
salt and pepper

one   Place a large saucepan of water on to boil for the spaghetti.

two   Remove all the meat from the lobster and cut it in to chunks.

three   Heat the oil in a saucepan, add the shallots and sauté for 3 minutes. Add the tomatoes and lemon juice, season with salt and pepper and cook for a further 3 minutes.

four   Place the spaghetti in the boiling water, stir and cook for 3–4 minutes if fresh or 8 minutes if dried, or according to packet instructions.

five   Add the lobster to the tomato sauce, stir, reduce the heat and cook for 4 minutes.

six   Drain the pasta well. Add the sauce to the pasta with the chopped chives, toss with two wooden spoons and serve immediately.

This dish makes an excellent quick supper to serve to friends – the addition of lobster makes it really special.

Preparation time **10 minutes**   Cooking time **15 minutes**
Total time **25 minutes**   *Serves 4*

pappardelle with prosciutto and porcini

Fresh or dried porcini may be used for this recipe. If you use dried porcini, use 125 g/4 oz and soak them in hot water for 15 minutes to rehydrate.

2 tablespoons olive oil
1 garlic clove, crushed and chopped
250 g/8 oz porcini, sliced
250 g/8 oz prosciutto
300 g/10 oz pappardelle
150 ml/¼ pint whipping cream
handful of flat leaf parsley, chopped
75 g/3 oz Parmesan cheese,
freshly grated
salt and pepper

one   Place a large saucepan of water on to boil for the pappardelle.

two   Heat the olive oil in a saucepan, add the garlic and porcini and sauté for 4 minutes over a moderate heat.

three   Cut the prosciutto in to strips; try and keep them separate.

four   Place the pappardelle in the boiling water and cook for 4 minutes if fresh and 9 minutes if dried, or according to packet instructions. Test a piece before draining.

five   Add the prosciutto, cream and parsley to the porcini and season with salt and pepper. Bring to the boil and simmer for 1 minute.

six   Add the pappardelle to the sauce and toss well using two spoons to mix evenly. Sprinkle with the Parmesan, toss well and serve at once.

Preparation time **10 minutes**
Cooking time **15 minutes**
Total time **25 minutes**   *Serves 4*

spaghetti carbonara

The true Italian way to serve spaghetti carbonara is with an egg yolk in its shell on top of each serving, which is mixed in by the person eating.

one   Heat the oil in a saucepan, add the bacon and cook gently for 3 minutes. Add the garlic and cook for 1 minute.

two   Place a large saucepan of water on to boil for the spaghetti. When it is boiling, add the spaghetti and cook for 3–4 minutes if fresh, or 8 minutes if dried, or according to packet instructions. Remove a piece and test. Drain when cooked and return to the pan.

three   Beat the cream and egg yolks together, add to the bacon and mix well over a low heat.

four   Add the sauce and Parmesan to the spaghetti, season with salt and pepper and toss well with two spoons. Mix well and serve immediately.

1 tablespoon olive oil
175 g/6 oz smoked bacon, rinded and cut in to strips
1 garlic clove, crushed and chopped
300 g/10 oz spaghetti
4 tablespoons double cream
3 egg yolks
75 g/3 oz Parmesan cheese, freshly grated
salt and pepper

Preparation time **10 minutes**   Cooking time **10 minutes**   Total time **20 minutes**   *Serves 4*

penne with chicken livers

1 yellow pepper, cored, halved and deseeded
300 g/10 oz penne
2 tablespoons olive oil
50 g/2 oz butter
1 red onion, sliced
250 g/8 oz chicken livers, trimmed
sprig of rosemary, chopped
salt and pepper
75 g/3 oz Parmesan cheese, freshly grated, to serve

one   Place a large saucepan of water on to boil for the pasta.

two   Roast the yellow pepper in a hot oven or under the grill for 5 minutes until the skin is blistered and black. Allow to cool then peel away the skin. Cut the flesh in to long strips.

three   Add the pasta to the boiling water and cook for 4 minutes if fresh and 8 minutes if dried, or according to packet instructions.

four   Heat the oil and butter in a large frying pan, add the onion and chicken livers and cook on a high heat until browned all over. Add the rosemary and season with salt and pepper. Do not overcook the chicken livers as this dries them out and makes them hard; they are best still pink in the middle.

five   Mix the chicken liver sauce with the pasta and toss well. Serve immediately with a bowl of freshly grated Parmesan.

Preparation time **15 minutes**   Cooking time **15 minutes**
Oven temperature **200°C (400°F), Gas Mark 6**
Total time **30 minutes**   *Serves 4*

pasta bake with spinach and ham

2 tablespoons olive oil
1 onion, chopped
1 garlic clove, crushed and chopped
750 g/1½ lb fresh spinach, washed and chopped
pinch of grated nutmeg
8 sheets fresh lasagne
250 g/8 oz ham, chopped in to large chunks
125 g/4 oz packet buffalo mozzarella cheese, thinly sliced
125 g/4 oz fontina cheese, grated
salt and pepper

one   Heat the olive oil in a saucepan, add the onion and garlic and sauté for 3 minutes.

two   Add the spinach and mix well, cook for 2 minutes over a moderate heat, just so that the spinach starts to wilt. Add nutmeg, to taste and season with salt and pepper.

three   Lightly oil a large shallow baking dish, place a layer of lasagne at the bottom, followed by a layer of spinach, then ham and then a layer of mozzarella. Repeat until all the ingredients are used, finishing with lasagne and the grated fontina cheese.

four   Place the dish at the top of a preheated oven, 200°C (400°F), Gas Mark 6, and bake for 15 minutes until golden brown and bubbling.

Preparation time **5 minutes**   Cooking time **20 minutes**
Total time **25 minutes**   *Serves 4*

orecchiette with spicy tomato and pancetta sauce

2 tablespoons olive oil
1 onion, chopped
2 garlic cloves, crushed and chopped
125 g/4 oz pancetta, chopped
400 g/13 oz can chopped tomatoes
½–1 teaspoon crushed dried chillies
125 ml/4 fl oz red wine
300 g/10 oz orecchiette
handful of flat leaf parsley, chopped
handful of basil, chopped
salt and pepper
75 g/3 oz Parmesan shavings, to garnish

one   Heat the olive oil in a saucepan, add the onion, garlic and pancetta and sauté for 5 minutes.

two   Add the chopped tomatoes, dried chillies and red wine and simmer for 15 minutes or until the sauce is rich and thick.

three   Place a large saucepan of water on to boil for the pasta.

four   Put the pasta in the boiling water, stir well and simmer for 3 minutes if fresh and 6 minutes if dried, or according to packet instructions. Drain well.

five   Stir the parsley, basil and salt and pepper in to the sauce. Add to the pasta and toss well. Garnish with some of the Parmesan shavings and serve with a separate bowl at the table.

Because this dish uses fresh lasagne and is loosely layered, it cooks through much more quickly than traditional baked lasagne.

Risotto

Traditionally risotto is served in small portions in large wide-rimmed soup plates and topped with grated Parmesan or pecorino cheese. Sometimes risottos are simple with just the addition of fresh herbs, other times they are more substantial, cooked with seafood, meat or vegetables. It is essential that the short-grained arborio or carnaroli rices are used for risottos.

Preparation time **10 minutes**   Cooking time **20 minutes**   Total time **30 minutes**   *Serves 4*

green vegetable risotto

1 litre/1¾ pints chicken or vegetable stock
125 g/4 oz butter
1 tablespoon olive oil
1 garlic clove, crushed and chopped
1 onion, finely diced
300 g/10 oz arborio or carnaroli rice
125 g/4 oz green beans, trimmed and cut in to
2.5 cm/1 inch pieces
125 g/4 oz shelled peas
125 g/4 oz shelled and skinned broad beans
125 g/4 oz asparagus, trimmed and cut in to
2.5 cm/1 inch pieces
125 g/4 oz baby spinach, washed and chopped
75 ml/3 fl oz dry vermouth or white wine
2 tablespoons chopped parsley
125 g/4 oz Parmesan cheese, freshly grated
salt and pepper

one   Place the chicken or vegetable stock in a saucepan and simmer gently.

two   Melt 50 g/2 oz of the butter with the olive oil in a heavy-based saucepan, add the garlic and onion, and sauté gently for 5 minutes; do not brown.

three   Add the rice, stir well to coat each grain with the butter and oil. Add enough stock to just cover the rice, stir again and simmer gently, stirring as frequently as possible.

four   When most of the liquid is absorbed, add more stock; keep adding stock, stirring and simmering gently until the stock is absorbed. When you add the last of the stock, add the vegetables and vermouth or white wine, mix well and cook for 2 minutes.

five   Remove the pan from the heat, season with salt and pepper and add the remaining butter, the chopped parsley and Parmesan. Mix well and serve at once.

Preparation time **5 minutes**   Cooking time **20 minutes**   Total time **25 minutes**   *Serves 4*

risotto alla Milanese

one   Place the chicken stock in a saucepan and simmer gently.

two   Melt 50 g/2 oz of the butter and the olive oil in a large heavy-based saucepan, add the onions and sauté for 5 minutes.

three   Add the rice to the onions and stir well to coat each grain with the butter; add enough stock to just cover the rice and stir well. Simmer gently, stirring as frequently as possible.

four   When most of the liquid is absorbed, add more stock and the saffron and stir well. Continue adding the stock in stages, and stirring until it has all been absorbed.

five   Finally add the vermouth or white wine, Parmesan and the remaining butter in small knobs and season with salt and pepper. Stir well and serve immediately.

1 litre/1¾ pints chicken stock
75 g/3 oz butter
1 tablespoon olive oil
2 onions, finely diced
425 g/14 oz arborio or carnaroli rice
½ teaspoon saffron threads
125 ml/4 fl oz dry vermouth or dry
white wine
125 g/4 oz Parmesan cheese,
freshly grated
salt and pepper

Fresh or dried mushrooms may be used for this recipe. If you use dried mushrooms, use 125 g/4 oz and soak them in hot water for 15 minutes to rehydrate. Use the excess liquid as stock in the recipe, as it is full of delicious flavours.

Preparation time **5 minutes**   Cooking time **20 minutes**   Total time **25 minutes**   *Serves 4*

risotto with forest mushrooms and sage

1 litre/1¾ pints vegetable stock
125 g/4 oz butter
1 tablespoon olive oil
1 garlic clove, crushed and chopped
1 onion, finely diced
250 g/8 oz forest (wild) mushrooms,
e.g. morel, porcini, chanterelle
or common open mushroom,
halved or quartered
300 g/10 oz arborio or carnaroli rice
75 ml/3 fl oz dry white wine
1 tablespoon chopped sage
salt and pepper
125 g/4 oz Parmesan cheese,
freshly grated, to serve
truffle oil, to drizzle (optional)

one   Pour the stock in to a saucepan and simmer gently.

two   Heat half the butter with the oil in a heavy-based saucepan, add the garlic and onion and sauté gently for 3 minutes; do not brown.

three Add the mushrooms to the onions and continue to cook gently for 2 minutes.

four   Add the rice and mix well so that all the grains are coated in the oil and butter.

five   Add just enough stock to cover the rice, stir well and simmer gently, stirring as frequently as possible throughout cooking. As the liquid evaporates, continue adding ladles of stock to just cover the rice, and stirring well.

six   Finally add the white wine, the remaining butter, the sage and salt and pepper to the rice and stir well. Serve with the Parmesan in a separate bowl and drizzle with truffle oil, if liked.

Preparation time **5 minutes**   Cooking time **20 minutes**
Total time **25 minutes**   *Serves 4*

red wine risotto

600 ml/1 pint chicken stock
450 ml/¾ pint Valpolicella or other
red wine
1 tablespoon olive oil
125 g/4 oz butter
2 garlic cloves, crushed and
chopped
2 red onions, chopped
300 g/10 oz arborio or carnaroli rice
250 g/8 oz field mushrooms, sliced
175 g/6 oz Parmesan cheese,
freshly grated
salt and pepper

one   Heat the stock and red wine in a large saucepan to a gentle simmer.

two   Heat the olive oil and 50 g/2 oz of the butter in a heavy-based saucepan, add the garlic and onions and sauté gently for 5 minutes; do not brown.

three Add the rice and mix well to coat the grains with the butter and oil. Add enough of the hot stock to cover the rice, stir well and simmer gently. Continue to stir as frequently as possible throughout cooking. As the liquid is absorbed, add more stock by the ladle to just cover the rice, stirring well.

four   When half of the stock has been incorporated, add the mushrooms and season with salt and pepper. The rice should be stained with the colour of the wine, giving it a rich dark red colour.

five   When all the stock has been added, and the rice is just cooked with a good creamy sauce, add most of the Parmesan and the remaining butter and mix well. Garnish with a little grated Parmesan and serve with the rest of the bottle of red wine.

Preparation time **5 minutes**   Cooking time **25 minutes**
Oven Temperature: **220°C (425°F), Gas Mark 7**   Total time **30 minutes**   *Serves 4*

butternut squash risotto

1 butternut squash, weighing 1 kg/2 lb
3 tablespoons olive oil
1 litre/1¾ pints chicken or vegetable stock
125 g/4 oz butter
1 garlic clove, crushed and chopped
1 onion, finely diced
300 g/10 oz arborio or carnaroli rice
150 g/5 oz Parmesan cheese, freshly grated
salt and pepper
pumpkin seed oil, to serve

one   Top and tail the squash, cut in half round the middle, then pare away the skin from the larger half without losing too much of the flesh. Cut in half lengthways, remove the seeds and cut in to 5 cm/2 inch dice. Repeat with the other half. Place on a large baking sheet, drizzle with 2 tablespoons of the olive oil and season with salt and pepper. Mix well and cook in the top of a preheated oven, 220°C (425°F), Gas Mark 7, for 15 minutes. The squash should be soft and slightly browned.

two   Meanwhile, heat the stock to a gentle simmer in a saucepan.

three Melt the remaining olive oil and 50 g/2 oz of the butter in a heavy-based saucepan, add the garlic and onion and sauté gently for 5 minutes; do not brown.

four   Add the rice, stir well to coat the grains with oil and butter, then add enough stock to cover the rice. Stir well and simmer gently. Continue to stir as frequently as possible throughout cooking. As the liquid is absorbed, continue adding ladlefuls of stock to just cover the rice, and stirring well.

five   Remove the squash from the oven, add to the risotto with the Parmesan and the remaining butter, season with salt and pepper and stir gently.

six   Serve the risotto on individual warmed plates with a little pumpkin seed oil drizzled on top of each portion.

Preparation time **5 minutes**   Cooking time **20 minutes**   Total time **25 minutes**   *Serves 4*

green herb risotto

1 litre/1¾ pints chicken or vegetable stock
125 g/4 oz butter
2 tablespoons olive oil
1 onion, finely chopped
1 garlic clove, crushed and chopped
300 g/10 oz arborio or carnaroli rice
handful of parsley, chopped
handful of basil, chopped
handful of oregano, chopped
handful of thyme, chopped
125 g/4 oz Toma cheese, grated
salt and pepper
herb sprigs, to garnish

one   Heat the stock in a saucepan to a gentle simmer.

two   Melt 50 g/2 oz of the butter with the olive oil in a saucepan, add the onion and garlic and sauté for 3 minutes.

three Add the rice, stir well to coat the grains with the butter and oil, then add a ladle of stock, enough to cover the rice, and stir well. Simmer gently and continue to stir as frequently as possible, adding more stock as it is absorbed. Continue adding the stock and stirring until it has all been absorbed and the rice is cooked with a rich creamy sauce.

four   Add the herbs, the remaining butter and the cheese. Season with salt and pepper and stir well. Serve immediately, garnished with the herb sprigs.

Toma cheese is made in the Italian Alps. If you cannot find it, use fontina or Parmesan instead.

Preparation time **5 minutes**   Cooking time **20 minutes**   Total time **25 minutes**   *Serves 4*

spinach and lemon risotto

1 litre/1¾ pints chicken or vegetable stock
125 g/4 oz butter
1 tablespoon olive oil
2 shallots, finely chopped
300 g/10 oz arborio or carnaroli rice
500 g/1 lb spinach, chopped
grated rind and juice of 1 lemon
125 g/4 oz Parmesan cheese, freshly grated
salt and pepper
grated lemon rind, to garnish (optional)

one   Heat the stock in a saucepan to a gentle simmer.

two   Melt 50 g/2 oz of the butter and the olive oil in a saucepan, add the shallots and sauté for 3 minutes.

three   Add the rice and stir well to coat the grains thoroughly with butter and oil. Add a ladleful of stock, enough to cover the rice, and stir well. Simmer gently and continue to stir as frequently as possible, adding more stock as it is absorbed.

four   Before you add the last of the stock, stir in the chopped spinach, lemon rind and juice and season with salt and pepper. Increase the heat, stir well then add the remaining stock and butter. Allow to cook for a few minutes, then add half of the Parmesan and mix in well. Serve garnished with the remaining Parmesan and grated lemon rind, if liked.

Preparation time **10 minutes**   Cooking time **20 minutes**
Total time **30 minutes**   *Serves 4*

seafood risotto

1 litre/1¾ pints fish, chicken or vegetable stock
good pinch of saffron threads
125 g/4 oz butter
2 tablespoons olive oil
3 shallots, chopped
1 garlic clove, crushed and chopped
300 g/10 oz arborio or carnaroli rice
125 g/4 oz small scallops, removed from their shells
125 g/4 oz prepared squid, cut in to rings
125 g/4 oz peeled prawns
2 tablespoons roughly chopped flat leaf parsley
75 ml/3 fl oz white wine or dry vermouth
125 g/4 oz Parmesan cheese, freshly grated
salt and pepper

one   Heat the stock and saffron in a saucepan to a gentle simmer.

two   Melt 50 g/2 oz of the butter and 1 tablespoon of the olive oil in another saucepan, add the shallots and garlic and sauté for 5 minutes; do not let them brown.

three   Add the rice and stir well to coat the grains thoroughly with the butter and oil. Pour in enough hot stock to cover the rice, stir well and simmer gently. Continue stirring as frequently as possible throughout the cooking. As the liquid is absorbed, add more stock by the ladle to just cover the rice, and stir well.

four   When half of the stock has been incorporated, add the scallops, squid and prawns, turn the heat up a little and continue to add the stock by the ladle; stir carefully so as not to break up the seafood.

five   When all the stock has been absorbed, add the parsley, the remaining butter, white wine or vermouth, half of the Parmesan and season with salt and pepper. Stir well. Serve garnished with the remaining Parmesan.

The secret of a good risotto is to cook it very slowly over a low heat until all the liquid has been absorbed and the rice is plump and tender.

Pizza
and Polenta

Naples is reputed to be the
original home of the pizza,
but pizzas are now found
all over Italy. Polenta is a
yellow maize flour from
northern Italy which can
be baked, grilled, used as
an accompaniment or is
delicious with the addition
of cheese.

Preparation time **10 minutes**   Cooking time **see recipes**   *Makes 4*

quick pizza base

250 g/8 oz self-raising flour
1 teaspoon salt
150 ml/¼ pint warm water

It is very important to cook the pizza bases in a very hot oven, so do make sure to turn the oven on well in advance when you come to cook the pizzas.

one   Place the flour and salt in a large bowl and mix well. Slowly add the water and mix to form a soft dough. When it has bound together, mix the dough with your hands in to a ball. Turn the dough out on a lightly floured surface and knead until smooth and soft.

two   Divide the dough in to 4 and with your hands and a rolling pin flatten it as thinly as possible. The pizza rounds do not have to be exact circles as that is one of the charms of making your own pizzas! Make the pizzas just a bit smaller than your serving plates and as thin as you can.

Preparation time **8–10 minutes, plus preparing the pizza base**   Cooking time **10 minutes**
Oven temperature **230°C (450°F), Gas Mark 8**   Total time **30 minutes**   *Serves 4*

classic tomato pizza

1 recipe Quick Pizza Base (see above)
3 tablespoons olive oil
2 red onions, sliced finely
2 garlic cloves, crushed and chopped
2 x 400 g/13 oz cans chopped tomatoes
1 teaspoon red wine vinegar
sugar, to taste
8 anchovy fillets, cut in to thin lengths
2 tablespoons pitted black olives
1 tablespoon capers
250 g/8 oz mozzarella cheese, sliced
salt and pepper

one   Roll out the dough to four circles or a large square.

two   Heat the oil in a large saucepan, add the onion and garlic and sauté for 3 minutes. Add the tomatoes, vinegar and sugar and season with salt and pepper. Increase the heat and simmer the mixture until it has reduced by half to make a thick and rich tomato sauce.

three   Place the pizza bases on warmed baking sheets, spoon over the sauce and spread to the edge with the back of the spoon.

four   Arrange the anchovies on the pizzas, sprinkle with the olives and capers and finally add the mozzarella. Put the pizzas in to a preheated oven, 230°C (450°F), Gas Mark 8, and cook for 10 minutes until golden and sizzling.

If you do not have enough baking sheets or space in your oven, make a large square pizza and serve it cut in to squares.

Preparation time **8–10 minutes**, plus preparing the pizza base
Cooking time **10–15 minutes**   Oven temperature **230°C (450°F), Gas Mark 8**
Total time **30 minutes**   *Serves 4*

fresh wild mushroom pizza

1 recipe Quick Pizza Base (see page 50)
olive oil, for brushing
2 onions, finely sliced
2 garlic cloves, crushed and chopped
250 g/8 oz wild mushrooms, sliced
drizzle of truffle oil
salt and pepper
handful of flat leaf parsley, chopped, to garnish

one   Put the pizza bases on to warmed baking sheets and brush them lightly with olive oil.

two   Mix together the onions, garlic and mushrooms and season with salt and pepper. Spread the mixture over the pizzas and drizzle with a scant amount of truffle oil. Put the pizzas in to a preheated oven, 230°C (450°F), Gas Mark 8, and bake for 10–15 minutes.

three   Sprinkle the pizzas with parsley and serve at once.

Preparation time **8–10 minutes**, plus preparing the pizza base
Cooking time **10–15 minutes**
Oven temperature **230°C (450°F), Gas Mark 8**
Total time **30 minutes**   *Serves 4*

artichoke and goats' cheese pizza

1 recipe Quick Pizza Base
(see page 50)
2 onions, sliced finely
1 kg/2 lb artichokes in oil
2 tablespoons pitted black olives
175 g/6 oz mild goats' cheese,
cut in to thin slices or
crumbled
handful of oregano, chopped
salt and pepper

one   Put the pizza bases on to warmed baking sheets.

two   Mix together the onions and artichokes and season well with salt and pepper.

three   Divide the mixture between the bases and spread over evenly. Sprinkle with the olives and top with the goats' cheese, oregano and salt and pepper. Put the pizzas in a preheated oven, 230°C (450°F), Gas Mark 8, and bake for 10–15 minutes.

The addition of 50 g/2 oz of wild mushrooms, such as chanterelles, to this pizza makes it really special.

Preparation time **20 minutes, plus preparing the pizza base** Cooking time **10 minutes**
Oven temperature **230°C (450°F), Gas Mark 8** Total time **30 minutes** *Serves 4*

fresh vegetable pizza

1 recipe Quick Pizza Base (see page 50)
5 tablespoons olive oil
2 garlic cloves, crushed and chopped
1 red onion, finely sliced
2 courgettes, thinly sliced lengthways
1 red pepper, cored, deseeded and cut in to thin strips
1 yellow pepper, cored, deseeded and cut in to thin strips
4 plum tomatoes, skinned, cored and cut in to small wedges
500 g/1 lb asparagus, trimmed
4 thyme sprigs, separated in to leaves
handful of basil leaves, roughly torn
salt and pepper
75 g/3 oz fresh Parmesan shavings (optional), to serve

one Put the pizza bases on to warmed baking sheets, brush with a little olive oil, then arrange the vegetables on the bases, sprinkling them with the thyme leaves and roughly torn basil.

two Season the pizzas generously with salt and pepper, drizzle with olive oil and bake at the top of a preheated oven, 230°C (450°F), Gas Mark 8, for 10 minutes. The vegetables should be slightly charred around the edges as this adds to the flavour. Serve with fresh Parmesan shavings, if liked.

Preparation time **8 minutes, plus preparing the pizza base** Cooking time **10 minutes**
Oven temperature **230°C (450°F), Gas Mark 8** Total time **18 minutes** *Serves 4*

anchovy and red pepper pizza

one Heat the olive oil in a saucepan, add the onions and red peppers and cook for about 5 minutes until soft. Add the garlic and mix well.

two Put the pizza bases on to warmed baking sheets and spoon and spread the cooked peppers over them. Arrange the anchovies on top and sprinkle with salt and pepper, chopped marjoram and olives and add the slices of mozzarella.

three Put the pizzas in to a preheated oven, 230°C (450°F), Gas Mark 8, and bake for 10 minutes.

4 tablespoons olive oil
2 red onions, sliced
4 red peppers, cored, deseeded and cut in to strips
2 garlic cloves, crushed and chopped
1 recipe Quick Pizza Base (see page 50)
50 g/2 oz can anchovies
handful of marjoram, chopped
1 tablespoon black olives, pitted and chopped
250 g/8 oz buffalo mozzarella, sliced
salt and pepper

Preparation time **5 minutes** Cooking time **about 15 minutes**
Total time **20 minutes** *Serves 4*

creamed polenta
with dolcelatte and mascarpone

600 ml/1 pint water
150 g/5 oz quick cooking
polenta flour
50 g/2 oz butter
2 tablespoons olive oil
175 g/6 oz dolcelatte and
mascarpone torta
handful of oregano,
chopped
salt and pepper

one Heat the water to a gentle simmer, pour in the polenta and beat well for 1–2 minutes until it becomes a smooth paste.

two Turn the heat down and continue to cook the polenta until it thickens, stirring constantly so that it does not catch on the bottom of the pan or form a skin on the top; it needs to cook in this way for 6–8 minutes.

three When it is thick and cooked, add the salt and pepper, the butter and olive oil and mix well. The dolcelatte and mascarpone torta is very creamy and wet; break it up in to small pieces and add to the polenta with the oregano. Mix well.

four The polenta should now be the consistency of soft mashed potatoes. Serve on its own or with grilled chicken breasts.

Preparation time **15 minutes, plus preparing the pizza base**
Cooking time **13–15 minutes** Oven temperature **230°C (450°F), Gas Mark 8**
Total time **30 minutes** *Serves 4*

1 recipe Quick Pizza Base (see page 50)
olive oil, for brushing and drizzling
2 onions, finely sliced
2 garlic cloves, peeled and sliced
4 tomatoes, skinned and sliced
250 g/8 oz spinach, cooked and chopped
8 slices Parma ham, cut in to strips
1 tablespoon black olives, pitted and
chopped
4 eggs
salt and pepper

spinach, Parma ham and egg pizza

one Put the pizza bases on to warmed baking sheets. Brush them lightly with olive oil and season with salt and pepper.

two Mix together the onions, garlic, tomatoes, spinach, Parma ham and olives and spread over the bases, making a nest in the middle of each one for the egg.

three Drizzle the pizzas with olive oil and season with salt and pepper. Place in a preheated oven, 230°C (450°F), Gas Mark 8, and cook for 10 minutes, then remove from the oven and crack the eggs in to the nests. Return the pizzas to the oven for 3–5 minutes then serve immediately. If you like your egg hard, put it on the vegetable topping when it first goes in the oven.

Polenta has to be stirred continuously during cooking or it will become lumpy. Use instant or quick cooking polenta for these recipes.

Preparation time **10 minutes**
Cooking time **20 minutes**
Oven temperature **200°C (400°F)**, Gas Mark 6
Total time **30 minutes**   *Serves 4*

baked polenta with fontina

600 ml/1 pint water
150 g/5 oz quick cooking polenta
   flour
125 g/4 oz butter
handful of marjoram, chopped
200 g/7 oz fontina cheese, grated
salt and pepper
Sauce:
3 tablespoons olive oil
2 garlic cloves, crushed and chopped
1 onion, chopped
400 g/13 oz can chopped tomatoes
1 thyme sprig
1 teaspoon vinegar
1 teaspoon sugar

one   Heat the water to a gentle simmer, pour in the polenta flour and beat well for 1–2 minutes until it is a smooth paste.

two   Turn the heat down and continue to cook the polenta until it thickens, stirring constantly so that it does not catch on the bottom of the pan or form a skin on the top; it needs to cook in this way for 6–8 minutes.

three When the polenta is thick and cooked add the butter, chopped marjoram and season with salt and pepper. Mix well. Place the polenta on a chopping board, roll out to 1.5 cm/¾ inch thick and allow to set for 5 minutes. Alternatively, shape in to a loaf shape and slice in to 1.5 cm/¾ inch thick slices.

four   To make the sauce, heat the olive oil in a saucepan, add the garlic and onion and sauté for 3 minutes.

five   Add the tomatoes, thyme, vinegar and sugar. Season with salt and pepper and simmer for 10 minutes over a moderate to high heat until the tomatoes reduce to make a thick sauce.

six   Butter a shallow ovenproof dish, cut the polenta in to squares and line the bottom of the dish with half of the squares. Sprinkle over half of the grated fontina. Spoon over half of the sauce and top with the remaining polenta. Add the remaining sauce and the remaining grated fontina and bake in a preheated oven, 200°C (400°F), Gas Mark 6, for 10–15 minutes until the cheese is golden and the sauce bubbling.

Preparation time **5 minutes**   Cooking time **25 minutes**   Total time **30 minutes**   *Serves 4*

grilled polenta with asparagus and Parmesan

600 ml/1 pint water
150 g/5 oz quick cooking polenta flour
50 g/2 oz butter
500 g/1 lb asparagus, trimmed
3 tablespoons olive oil
1 tablespoon balsamic vinegar
salt and pepper
125 g/4 oz Parmesan shavings, to garnish

Parmesan shavings are best made with a mandoline, but you can also use a vegetable peeler. Shave the Parmesan straight on to the prepared dish as the shavings are very fragile and do not handle well.

one   Heat the water to a gentle simmer, pour in the polenta flour and beat well for 1–2 minutes until it is a smooth paste.

two   Turn the heat down and continue to cook the polenta until it thickens, stirring constantly so that it does not catch on the bottom of the pan or form a skin on the top; it needs to cook in this way for 6–8 minutes. When it is thick and cooked add the salt and pepper and the butter; mix well.

three Turn the polenta on to a chopping board, roll out to 1.5 cm/¾ inch thick and leave to set for 5 minutes.

four   A griddle pan or a grill can be used to finish this dish. Heat the griddle pan until it is hot or turn the grill on to full to heat up.

five   Cut the polenta in to wedges, and cook on each side for 5 minutes. If you are using a griddle it will be easier to get a good colour, but this does not affect the taste.

six   Grill or griddle the asparagus for 4–5 minutes on a high heat, turning it as it colours.

seven   To serve, arrange the polenta on a warmed serving dish and place the asparagus on top. Drizzle with the olive oil and balsamic vinegar and garnish with the Parmesan shavings.

Preparation time **10 minutes**   Cooking time **20 minutes**
Total time **30 minutes**   *Serves 4*

rich polenta salad

600 ml/1 pint water
150 g/5 oz quick cooking polenta flour
25 g/1 oz butter
250 g/8 oz goats' cheese, rind removed
1 small radicchio lettuce, separated in to leaves
125 g/4 oz rocket
3 tablespoons extra virgin olive oil
1 tablespoon balsamic vinegar
salt and pepper

one   Heat the water to a gentle simmer, pour in the polenta flour and beat well for 1–2 minutes until it is a smooth paste. Turn the heat down and continue to cook the polenta until it thickens, stirring constantly so that it does not catch on the bottom of the pan or form a skin on the top; it needs to cook in this way for 6–8 minutes.

two   When the polenta is thick and cooked add the butter and season with salt and pepper; mix well. Place it on a chopping board and spread to 1.5 cm/¾ inch thick and allow to set for 5 minutes.

three   Slice thinly or crumble the goats' cheese and arrange it on the polenta, then cut the polenta in to bars or wedges. Place the polenta under a preheated grill and cook until the cheese has melted and starts to bubble.

four   Put the radicchio leaves and the rocket in to a bowl. Add the oil and vinegar and season with salt and pepper, then toss the leaves until coated. Arrange the salad leaves on individual plates and place the polenta bars on top.

Preparation time **5 minutes**   Cooking time **25 minutes**   Total time **30 minutes**   *Serves 4*

grilled polenta with mushrooms and Parma ham

one   Heat the water to a gentle simmer, pour in the polenta flour and beat well for 1–2 minutes until it is a smooth paste.

two   Turn the heat down and continue to cook the polenta until it thickens, keep stirring constantly so that it does not catch on the bottom of the pan or form a skin on the top; it needs to cook in this way for 6–8 minutes.

three   When the polenta is thick and cooked, add 50 g/2 oz of the butter and season with salt and pepper; mix well. Turn the polenta on to a chopping board, roll out to 1.5 cm/¾ inch thick and leave to set for 5 minutes.

four   Melt the remaining butter in a saucepan with the olive oil. Add the garlic, mushrooms and thyme and sauté for 10 minutes with the wine, to keep them moist. Season with salt and pepper.

five   Cut the polenta in to wedges, place on a preheated griddle or under a hot grill and cook for 5 minutes on each side.

six   Serve the polenta with the Parma ham draped over and the mushrooms spooned over to one side. This dish can be served hot or at room temperature.

600 ml/1 pint water
150 g/5 oz quick cooking polenta flour
125 g/4 oz butter
1 tablespoons olive oil
1 garlic clove, crushed and chopped
375 g/12 oz mushrooms, sliced
½ teaspoon chopped thyme
125 ml/4 fl oz dry white wine
8 thin slices Parma ham
salt and pepper

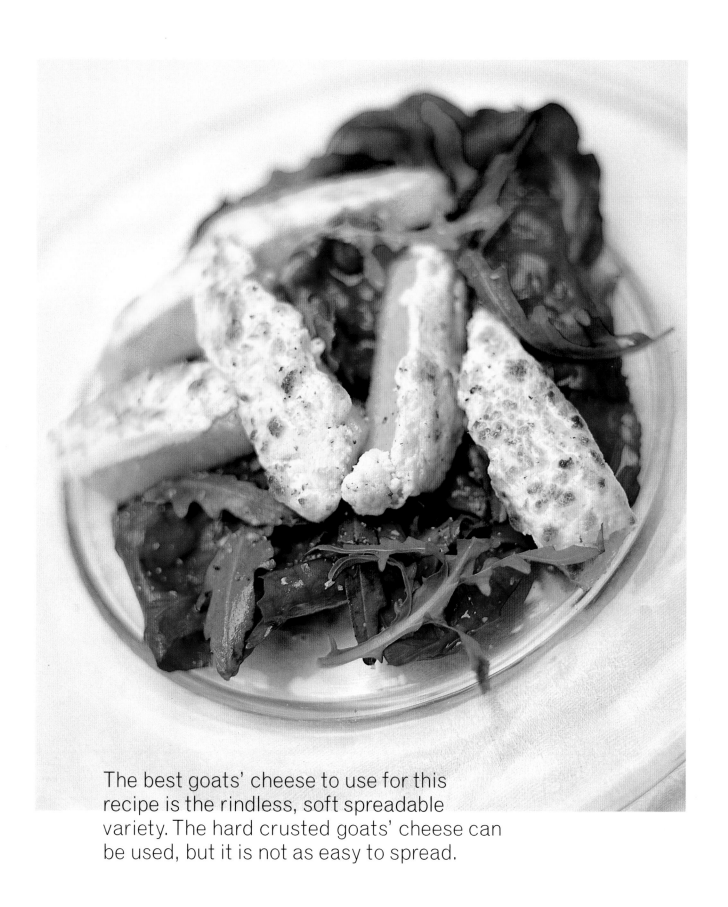

The best goats' cheese to use for this
recipe is the rindless, soft spreadable
variety. The hard crusted goats' cheese can
be used, but it is not as easy to spread.

Salads

The majority of
salads in this
chapter can be
main meals in their
own right, but
many make great
accompaniments
or starters too.

Preparation time **20 minutes**   Cooking time **5 minutes**
Total time **25 minutes**   *Serves 4*

Caesar salad

one   Place the garlic, anchovy fillets, lemon juice, mustard and egg yolk in a small mixing bowl and season with pepper. With a hand-held blender or small whisk, mix well until combined. Slowly drizzle in the olive oil, mixing all the time to form a thick creamy sauce. If the sauce is too thick, add a little water.

two   Heat the vegetable oil in a frying pan. Test with a small piece of bread to see if it is hot enough; if the bread sizzles add the croûtons, turning them when they are golden. When they are cooked, transfer them to a plate lined with kitchen paper to absorb the excess oil.

three   Put the lettuce in to a large bowl, pour over the dressing and 2 tablespoons of the Parmesan and mix well.

four   Serve the salad in a large bowl or on individual plates, sprinkle with the croûtons and the remaining Parmesan.

1 garlic clove, peeled and crushed
4 anchovy fillets, chopped
juice of 1 lemon
2 teaspoons dry English mustard
1 egg yolk
200 ml/7 fl oz extra virgin olive oil
vegetable oil for frying
3 slices country bread, cubed
1 Cos lettuce, washed and torn in to
    pieces
3 tablespoons freshly grated
    Parmesan cheese
pepper

Preparation time **15 minutes**   Total time **15 minutes**   *Serves 4*

panzanella

When making this delicious but very simple salad dish do try and cut all the ingredients in to a similar size. This salad makes a great starter or a side dish to serve with a summer fish supper.

one   Cut or tear the bread in to small pieces and place them in a large bowl.

two   Remove the green core from the tomatoes. Cut them up and add to the bread.

three   Cut the cucumber in quarters lengthways and then in to cubes. Add to the salad. Chop the onion and add to the bowl with the parsley and olives.

four   Mix together the olive oil, vinegar, lemon juice and season with salt and pepper. Pour the dressing over the salad and mix well. Cover and leave to stand at room temperature for at least 1 hour before serving, to allow all the flavours to steep and mingle.

4 slices ciabatta bread
4 ripe tomatoes
½ cucumber, peeled
1 red onion
handful of chopped flat leaf parsley
1 tablespoon chopped black olives
4 tablespoons extra virgin olive oil
1–2 tablespoons wine vinegar
juice of ½ lemon
salt and pepper

All the ingredients for this dish can be prepared in advance, but never mix the salad until it is needed as the lettuce will go soggy.

Preparation time **10 minutes**   Cooking time **2 minutes**   Total time **12 minutes**   *Serves 4*

tomato and green bean salad

250 g/8 oz mixed red and yellow baby
tomatoes, plum if possible
250 g/8 oz thin green beans, topped and tailed
handful of mint, chopped
1 garlic clove, crushed and chopped
4 tablespoons extra virgin olive oil
1 tablespoons balsamic vinegar
salt and pepper

one   Cut the baby tomatoes in half and place in a large bowl.

two   Cook the green beans in boiling water for 2 minutes, then drain well and place in the large bowl with the tomatoes.

three   Add the chopped mint, garlic, olive oil and balsamic vinegar. Season with salt and pepper and mix well. Serve warm or cold.

white bean and sun-dried tomato salad

Preparation time **10 minutes**
Cooking time **5 minutes**
Total time **15 minutes**   *Serves 4*

one   Heat the oil in a frying pan, add the onion and garlic and sauté over a high heat, stirring, to gain a little colour. When they are golden, remove from the pan.

two   Put the beans in to a mixing bowl and stir in the onion and garlic. Add the sun-dried tomatoes, olives, capers, thyme, extra virgin olive oil, lemon juice and salt and pepper to taste and mix well. Check the seasoning and serve.

2 tablespoons olive oil
1 onion, sliced
1 garlic clove, crushed and chopped
425 g/14 oz can white beans, drained
125 g/4 oz sun-dried tomatoes in oil,
    drained and roughly chopped
1 tablespoon chopped black olives
2 teaspoons chopped capers
2 teaspoons chopped thyme
1 tablespoon extra virgin olive oil
juice of ½ lemon
salt and pepper

Preparation time **10 minutes**   Cooking time **2 minutes**   Total time **12 minutes**   *Serves 4*

new season broad bean and pecorino salad

375 g/12 oz shelled
fresh broad beans
175 g/6 oz pecorino
cheese
2 tablespoons extra
virgin olive oil
juice of ½ lemon
1 tablespoon chopped
flat leaf parsley
salt and pepper

one   Blanch the beans in boiling water for 2 minutes. Drain and refresh. If you have the time, after blanching the beans, remove the outer skins to reveal the bright green, velvety bean inside.

two   Grate the cheese on the coarse grid of the grater and put it in a mixing bowl. Add the beans, olive oil, lemon juice and parsley, season with salt and pepper and mix well. Serve as part of an antipasto.

This salad makes a tasty supper in its own right as well as being an ideal accompaniment to grilled meat or fish.

Preparation time **10 minutes**   Cooking time **10 minutes**
Oven temperature **190°C (375°F), Gas Mark 5**
Total time **20 minutes**   *Serves 4*

aubergine, tomato and mozzarella mountains

1 aubergine, cut in to 8 slices
4 beef tomatoes, skinned, then cut in to 8 slices
250 g/8 oz packet buffalo mozzarella, cut in to 8 slices
2 tablespoons olive oil
Pesto (see page 16)
salt and pepper
mint sprigs, to garnish

one   Arrange the aubergine slices on a preheated griddle or under a hot grill and cook until browned on both sides.

two   Lightly oil a baking sheet.

three   To prepare the stacks, place four of the aubergine slices on the baking sheet. Put a tomato slice and a mozzarella slice on each one, then make a second layer of aubergine, tomato and mozzarella, sprinkling each layer with salt and pepper as you go. Skewer with a cocktail stick through the centre to hold the stacks together.

four   Place the stacks in a preheated oven, 190°C (375°F), Gas Mark 5, and cook for 10 minutes.

five   To serve, transfer the stacks on to individual serving plates and carefully remove the cocktail sticks. Drizzle with a little olive oil and top with a generous spoonful of pesto. Garnish with mint sprigs and serve warm or at room temperature.

Preparation time **10 minutes**
Cooking time **20 minutes**
Total time **30 minutes**
Serves 4

caponata   This salad actually improves if left to stand.

6 tablespoons olive oil
2 aubergines, cubed
1 red onion, chopped
3 celery sticks, chopped
5 tomatoes, skinned and roughly chopped
3 tablespoons red wine vinegar
1 tablespoon sugar
1 tablespoon capers
50 g/2 oz black olives, pitted
handful of flat leaf parsley, chopped
salt and pepper

one   Heat the oil in a saucepan, add the aubergines and fry until golden and soft. Remove from the pan and drain on kitchen paper.

two   Add the onion and celery to the pan and sauté for 6 minutes until soft but not brown.

three   Add the tomatoes and cook for 3 minutes, then add the vinegar, sugar, capers, olives, parsley and season with salt and pepper. Simmer for 5 minutes. Remove the pan from the heat, add the aubergines and mix well. Allow to cool then serve.

Serve these 'mountains' with crusty Italian
bread to mop up the delicious pesto juices.

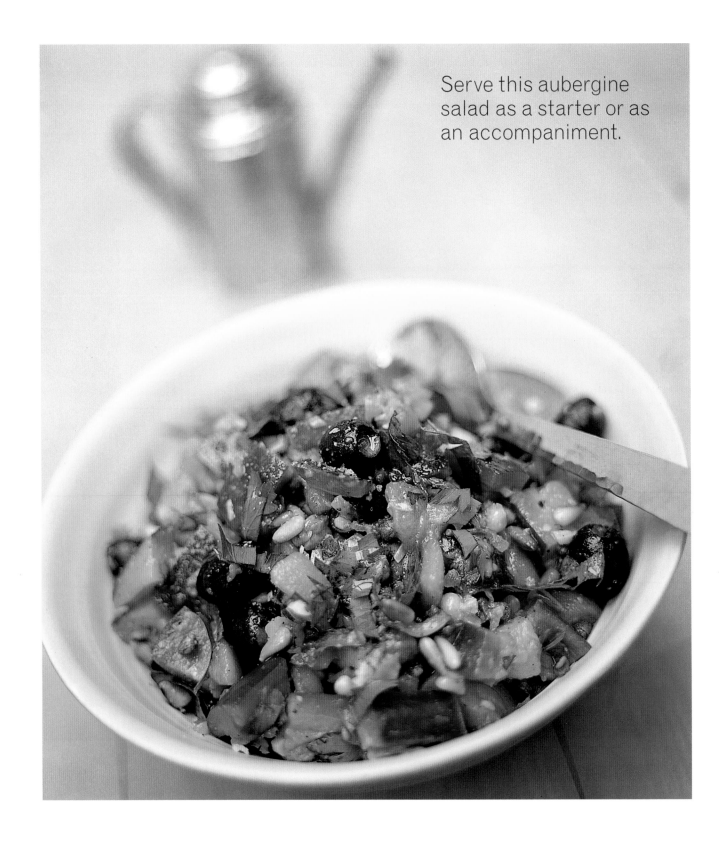

Serve this aubergine
salad as a starter or as
an accompaniment.

Preparation time **10 minutes, plus cooling**   Cooking time **15 minutes**
Total time **25 minutes**   *Serves 4*

aubergine salad

4 tablespoons olive oil
1 onion, chopped
2 garlic cloves, crushed and chopped
2 aubergines, cubed
4 tomatoes, peeled and roughly chopped
4 anchovy fillets, chopped
2 tablespoons pitted black olives
75 g/3 oz pine nuts, toasted
2 tablespoons chopped capers
handful of flat leaf parsley, chopped
salt and pepper
Italian salad dressing:
1 tablespoon white wine vinegar
3 tablespoons olive oil
juice of ½ lemon
1 teaspoon Dijon mustard

one   Heat the olive oil in a saucepan, add the onion, garlic and aubergines and sauté for 15 minutes.

two   Meanwhile, make the Italian salad dressing. Place all the ingredients in a jar with a lid, season with salt and pepper and shake well. Set aside.

three   Add the tomatoes, anchovies, olives, pine nuts, capers and parsley to the aubergine mixture and season with salt and pepper. Pour in the salad dressing, mix well then allow the salad to cool.

Preparation time **5 minutes, plus cooling**   Cooking time **25 minutes**
Oven temperature **200°C (400°F), Gas Mark 6**   Total time **30 minutes**   *Serves 4*

Piedmont peppers

4 red peppers
4–8 anchovy fillets
4 tomatoes, skinned and quartered
4 tablespoons olive oil
salt and pepper
To garnish:
handful of green or red basil, roughly torn
125 g/4 oz Parmesan cheese

one   Cut the peppers in half lengthways. Cut through the stalk first and then the flesh. I always leave the stalk on as it looks attractive. Remove the seeds and the white ribs.

two   Lightly oil a baking sheet and place the peppers on it, skin side down.

three   Cut the anchovies in to halves or quarters lengthways, depending how much you like anchovies.

four   Put 2 tomato quarters in to each red pepper, make an anchovy cross on top and drizzle with olive oil. Sprinkle with salt and pepper and place in a preheated oven, 200°C (400°F), Gas Mark 6, and cook for 25 minutes.

five   Allow the peppers to cool, then serve garnished with torn basil and Parmesan shavings. Shave the Parmesan straight on to the peppers, using a mandoline or a vegetable peeler, as it does not handle well.

Preparation time **15 minutes**
Total time **15 minutes**
Serves 4

rocket, tuna and haricot bean salad

4 tomatoes, skinned, cored and roughly chopped
125 g/4 oz rocket
425 g/14 oz can haricot beans, drained
200 g/7 oz can tuna in olive oil
1 red onion, chopped
125 g/4 oz artichoke hearts in olive oil
2 young celery sticks with leaves, chopped
1 tablespoon pitted black olives
juice of 1 lemon
1 tablespoon red wine vinegar
¼ teaspoon crushed dried chilli
handful of flat leaf parsley, roughly chopped
salt and pepper

one   Put the tomatoes in to a large salad bowl with the rocket.

two   Stir in the haricot beans and the tuna and olive oil, roughly breaking up the tuna in to large flakes. Stir in the chopped red onion.

three   Add the artichoke hearts and their olive oil, celery, olives, lemon juice, red wine vinegar, crushed dried chilli, parsley and season with salt and pepper.

four   Mix all the ingredients together well and allow to stand for 30 minutes for the flavours to mingle. Serve at room temperature with warm crusty bread.

Preparation time **10 minutes**   Cooking time **15 minutes**   Total time **25 minutes**   *Serves 4*

chicken and Parmesan salad

one   Place the chicken breasts on a hot griddle pan or under a preheated hot grill and cook on each side for 5 minutes.

two   Put the garlic, olive oil, anchovies, lemon juice, mustard and egg yolk in to a blender, season with pepper and mix until blended.

three   Put the Cos lettuce in to a large bowl, pour in the dressing and toss.

four   Arrange the lettuce on serving plates and sprinkle with torn basil leaves and the croûtons.

five   Slice the chicken in to long lengths and place on top of the lettuce. Shave the Parmesan on to the chicken with a mandoline or vegetable peeler and serve.

2 skinless, boneless chicken breasts
1 garlic clove, crushed and chopped
150 ml/¼ pint olive oil
3 anchovy fillets, roughly chopped
juice of ½ lemon
1 teaspoon English mustard powder
1 egg yolk
1 Cos lettuce, torn in to pieces
handful of basil, roughly torn
3 slices ciabatta or white country
    bread, cubed and fried in oil
75 g/3 oz Parmesan cheese
pepper

Preparation time **5 minutes, plus 5 minutes standing**
Total time **10 minutes** *Serves 4*

figs with Parma ham

4 figs
juice of ½ lemon
4 tablespoons extra virgin olive oil
handful of basil, roughly torn
12 slices Parma ham, cut in to paper-thin
    slices
salt and pepper

one   Cut the figs in to quarters and
remove the stems. Place them in a dish
with the lemon juice, olive oil, roughly
torn basil leaves and season with salt
and pepper. Mix well and allow to stand
for 5 minutes.

two   Arrange the Parma ham on a
serving plate then spoon the figs over the
ham. Sprinkle with salt and pepper and
serve at room temperature.

This recipe is very simple and relies heavily on
the quality of ingredients used, so it is best
made when figs are in season and then only if
they look ripe and delicious. It is also
important to buy your Parma ham from a
delicatessen where the ham is carved to order.
If you like, the figs can be replaced with a
fragrant, ripe melon, peeled, deseeded and cut
in to wedges.

Vegetables

In Italy, vegetables appear at many different stages of the meal, as antipasti, in soups, as accompaniments and as main courses. Italy is blessed with an abundance of different vegetables including baby artichokes, asparagus, spinach and fennel.

Preparation time **10 minutes**   Cooking time **10 minutes**   Total time **20 minutes**   *Serves 4*

quick spinach

1 tablespoon olive oil
1 red onion, sliced
1 garlic clove, crushed and chopped
75 g/3 oz pine nuts
4 tomatoes, peeled, cored and roughly chopped
1 kg/2 lb spinach, washed and trimmed
50 g/2 oz butter
pinch of nutmeg
salt and pepper

one   Heat the oil in a large saucepan, add the onion and garlic and sauté for 5 minutes.

two   Put the pine nuts in to a heavy-bottomed frying pan and dry-fry until browned, stirring all the time as they turn very quickly. Set aside.

three Add the tomatoes, spinach, butter, nutmeg and season with salt and pepper; turn up the heat to high and mix well. Cook for 3 minutes until the spinach has just started to wilt. Remove the pan from the heat, stir in the pine nuts and serve immediately.

If you have to wash the spinach do make sure that it is dry before you start to cook. Place it in a salad spinner or tea towel, and spin it around to disperse any excess water.

Preparation time **5 minutes**
Cooking time **10 minutes**
Total time **15 minutes**
Serves 4

fried courgettes with chillies

750 g/1½ lb courgettes, thickly sliced
75 g/3 oz plain flour
oil, for frying
50 g/2 oz butter
½ teaspoon crushed dried chillies
2 garlic cloves, crushed and chopped
juice and rind of 1 lemon
1 tablespoon green olives, pitted and chopped
salt and pepper

one   Dust the courgette slices all over with flour.

two   Heat the oil in a frying pan and fry the courgettes, in batches, for 2 minutes on each side, until golden. Remove from the pan and keep warm.

three When all the courgettes are cooked, pour off the oil from the pan. Add the butter, chillies, garlic, lemon juice and rind and the green olives and heat until the butter is foaming. Pour over the courgettes, season with salt and pepper and toss. Serve immediately.

Preparation time **10 minutes**   Cooking time **12 minutes**   Total time **22 minutes**   *Serves 4*

courgette fritters

500 g/1 lb courgettes, trimmed and grated
1 garlic clove, crushed and chopped
50 g/2 oz Parmesan cheese, freshly grated
50 g/2 oz plain flour
1 egg, beaten
olive oil, for frying
salt and pepper
1 lemon, cut in to 4 wedges, to serve

one   Mix together the grated courgettes, garlic, Parmesan, flour and beaten egg in a large bowl and season with salt and pepper.

two   Heat the olive oil in a frying pan. Place spoonfuls of the courgette mixture in the hot oil and fry for about 4–5 minutes on each side or until golden and crispy.

three As the fritters are done, lift them out of the pan with a slotted spoon and pile in a warmed serving dish and keep warm. Keep cooking until all the courgette mixture is used up.

four   Serve the fritters sprinkled with salt and accompanied by lemon wedges.

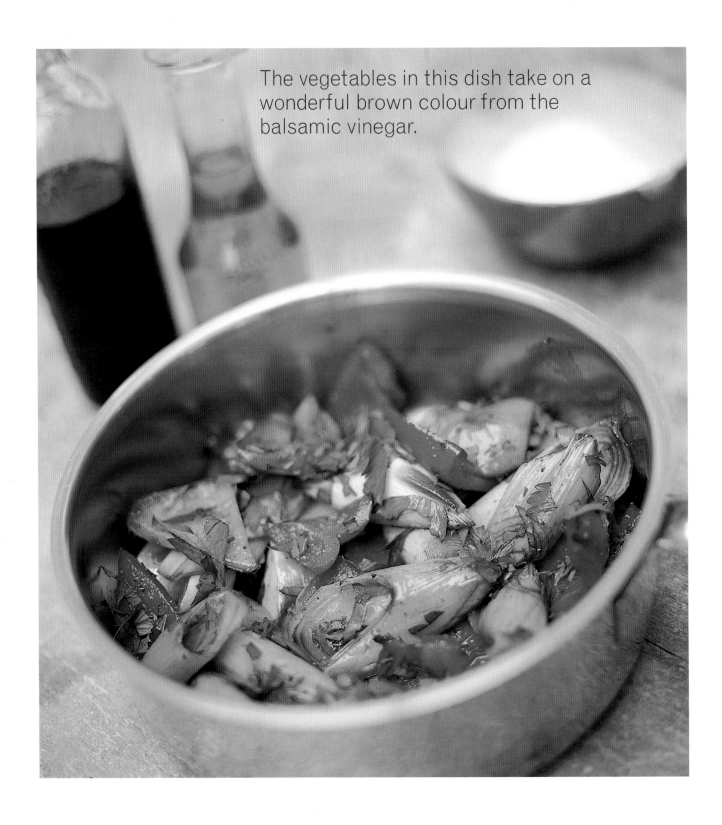

The vegetables in this dish take on a wonderful brown colour from the balsamic vinegar.

Preparation time **5 minutes**   Cooking time **20 minutes**   Total time **25 minutes**   *Serves 4*

balsamic braised leeks and peppers

2 tablespoons olive oil
2 leeks, cut in to 1 cm/½ inch pieces
1 orange pepper, cored, deseeded
and cut in to 1 cm/½ inch chunks
1 red pepper, cored, deseeded and
cut in to 1 cm/½ inch chunks
3 tablespoons balsamic vinegar
handful of flat leaf parsley, chopped
salt and pepper

one   Heat the olive oil in a saucepan, add the leeks and orange and red peppers, stir well, cover the pan and cook very gently for 10 minutes.

two   Add the balsamic vinegar and cook for a further 10 minutes without a lid. The vegetables should be brown from the vinegar and all the liquid should have evaporated.

three   Season well, and stir in the parsley just before serving.

Preparation time **5 minutes**   Cooking time **25 minutes**
Oven temperature **200°C (400°F), Gas Mark 6**
Total time **30 minutes**   *Serves 4–6*

vegetable frittata

There are many variations of frittata. Usually they are made with vegetables but try adding pancetta or chilli salami.

one   Heat the olive oil in a frying pan with a heat-proof handle. Add the onions, garlic, potatoes, red peppers and courgettes and sauté for 5 minutes.

two   Add the thyme, season with salt and pepper and mix well. Pour in the beaten eggs and cook over a moderate heat for 3 minutes.

three   Sprinkle with the grated Parmesan and put the pan in a preheated oven, 200°C (400°F), Gas Mark 6, and cook for 15 minutes. The frittata should be set and golden on top.

four   Remove the pan from the oven, ease a palette knife all the way round the edge and under the frittata, slide it on to a large plate and serve at once.

2 tablespoons olive oil
2 onions, finely sliced
2 garlic cloves, crushed and chopped
2 potatoes, boiled and sliced
2 red peppers, cored, deseeded and cut in to strips
6 courgettes, sliced
1 thyme sprig, chopped
5 eggs, beaten
50 g/2 oz Parmesan cheese, freshly grated
salt and pepper

Preparation time **5 minutes**   Cooking time **25 minutes**
Oven temperature **200°C (400°F), Gas Mark 6**
Total time **30 minutes**
Serves 4–6

spinach and ricotta frittata

2 tablespoons olive oil
2 onions, finely sliced
5 eggs
1 garlic clove, crushed and chopped
500 g/1 lb spinach, washed and chopped
175 g/6 oz ricotta cheese
50 g/2 oz pine nuts
25 g/1 oz black olives, pitted and chopped
salt and pepper

one   Heat the olive oil in a frying pan with a heat-proof handle, add the onions and garlic and sauté for 3 minutes; do not brown.

two   Beat the eggs in a large bowl; season well with salt and pepper, then add the chopped spinach and crumble in three-quarters of the ricotta. Add the pine nuts and olives and mix well. Add the onions and garlic and mix again.

three   Heat a little more oil in the frying pan, pour in the spinach mixture and cook for 5 minutes.

four   Sprinkle with the remaining ricotta, season with salt and pepper and place the pan in a preheated oven, 200°C (400°F), Gas Mark 6, for 15 minutes.

five   When cooked the frittata should be set and golden on top. To serve, ease a palette knife around the edge and underneath and slide the frittata on to a large plate. This dish can be eaten hot or cold.

Preparation time **5 minutes**
Cooking time **25 minutes**
Oven temperature **200°C (400°F), Gas Mark 6**
Total time **30 minutes**
Serves 4

fennel baked with cream and Parmesan

750 g/1½ lb fennel
small knob of butter
250 ml/8 fl oz double cream
75 g/3 oz freshly grated Parmesan cheese
salt and pepper

one   Trim the outside leaves from the fennel, remove the hard central core and slice the fennel lengthways. Immerse the leaves in a pan of boiling water and cook for 5 minutes. Drain well.

two   Butter a shallow ovenproof dish, add the fennel and sprinkle with salt and pepper. Pour over the cream and sprinkle with the Parmesan.

three   Place the dish at the top of a preheated oven, 200°C (400°F), Gas Mark 6, and cook for 20 minutes. Allow the top of the fennel to go a deep golden brown.

Preparation time **5 minutes**   Cooking time **25 minutes**
Oven temperature **220°C (425°F), Gas Mark 7**
Total time **30 minutes**   *Serves 4*

roast vegetables with olive oil and chillies

4 tablespoons olive oil
250 g/8 oz parsnips, cut in
to equal-size chunks
250 g/8 oz leeks, cut in to
1 cm/½ inch lengths
250 g/8 oz red peppers,
cored, deseeded and
cut in to squares
250 g/8 oz aubergines, cut
in to chunks
½ teaspoon crushed dried
chillies
handful of marjoram,
chopped
salt and pepper

one   Place the olive oil in a large roasting tin and put it in to a preheated oven, 220°C (425°F), Gas Mark 7, for a few minutes to warm.

two   Add the parsnips to the tin, toss well in the oil, then return the tin to the top of the oven and cook the parsnips for 10 minutes.

three Remove the tin from the oven and add the leeks, red peppers, aubergines and crushed chillies. Toss to coat in the olive oil then return the tin to the oven to cook for a further 15 minutes.

four   Remove the tin from the oven, add the chopped marjoram and salt and pepper to the vegetables; mix well and serve immediately.

Preparation time **5 minutes**   Cooking time **20 minutes**   Oven temperature **200°C (400°F), Gas Mark 6**
Total time **25 minutes**   *Serves 4*

baked young celery with Parmesan

This recipe also works very well with fennel.

one   Butter a large ovenproof dish. Cut the celery heads in to quarters lengthways and place in the prepared dish. Add the oregano, drizzle with olive oil and season well with salt and pepper.

two   Sprinkle the grated Parmesan over the celery and cook in a preheated oven, 200°C (400°F), Gas Mark 6, for 20 minutes. The celery should become soft and the cheese golden and crunchy on top.

25 g/1 oz butter
2 small young heads of celery
handful of oregano, chopped
3 tablespoons olive oil
75 g/3 oz Parmesan cheese, freshly grated
salt and pepper

Preparation time **5 minutes**   Cooking time **25 minutes**
Oven temperature **190°C (375°F), Gas Mark 5**   Total time **30 minutes**   *Serves 4*

baked aubergine and Gorgonzola

4 tablespoons olive oil
1 red onion, chopped
2 garlic cloves, crushed and chopped
400 g/13 oz can chopped tomatoes
1 red chilli, diced
handful of basil, roughly torn
2 aubergines, thickly sliced
125 g/4 oz Gorgonzola cheese
salt and pepper

one   Heat 1 tablespoon of the olive oil in a saucepan and sauté the onion and garlic for 3 minutes.

two   Add the tomatoes and chilli and simmer for aboout 8–10 minutes until the sauce has reduced. Add the basil and season well with salt and pepper.

three   Heat the remaining olive oil in a large frying pan, add the aubergine slices and fry until golden on each side.

four   Place a layer of aubergines in a shallow ovenproof dish and spoon over half of the sauce. Make another layer of aubergines, then add the rest of the sauce and finally crumble over the Gorgonzola. Bake in a preheated oven, 190°C (375°F), Gas Mark 5, for 15 minutes.

Preparation time **5 minutes**   Cooking time **25 minutes**
Oven temperature **200°C (400°F), Gas Mark 6**
Total time **30 minutes**   *Serves 4*

stuffed aubergines

2 aubergines
4 tablespoons olive oil
8 tomatoes, skinned and chopped
2 garlic cloves, crushed and chopped
4 anchovy fillets, chopped
1 tablespoon capers, chopped
handful of basil, chopped
handful of flat leaf parsley, chopped
75 g/3 oz pecorino cheese, grated
2 tablespoons pine nuts, toasted (see opposite)
50 g/2 oz white breadcrumbs
salt and pepper

one   Cut the aubergines in half lengthways and scoop out the flesh without breaking the skin. Roughly chop the flesh.

two   Heat the olive oil in a frying pan, add the aubergine shells and sauté them on each side for 3–4 minutes. Place them in a lightly oiled baking dish and sauté the flesh until golden brown.

three   Mix together the chopped tomato, garlic, anchovies, capers, basil, parsley, half of the pecorino cheese, the pine nuts, breadcrumbs and aubergine flesh and season with salt and pepper. Spoon the mixture in to the sautéed aubergine shells, piling it high. Sprinkle with the remaining cheese, then place in a preheated oven, 200°C (400°F), Gas Mark 6, and cook for 20 minutes.

These aubergines are delicious and can be served hot or cold. If you prefer, peppers and courgettes can be used instead.

Sicilian aubergines

one   Heat the olive oil in a heavy-bottomed saucepan, add the onions, garlic and celery and sauté for 3 minutes.

two   Add the aubergine and yellow and red peppers, turn up the heat and cook for a further 5 minutes, stirring constantly.

three   Add the passata and vinegar and bring to the boil, then reduce the heat so that the mixture just simmers for 10 minutes. Add the anchovies, capers and olives and simmer the mixture for a further 5 minutes.

four   Meanwhile, put the pine nuts in to a heavy-bottomed pan and dry-fry until browned, stirring all the time as they turn very quickly.

five   Finally season the aubergine mixture with pepper, add the pine nuts and chopped parsley and mix well. Serve hot or at room temperature.

4 tablespoons olive oil
2 red onions, sliced
2 garlic cloves, crushed and
    chopped
2 celery sticks, chopped
1 aubergine, cut in to small dice
1 yellow pepper, cored, deseeded
    and cut in to thin strips
1 red pepper, cored, deseeded and
    cut in to thin strips
150 ml/¼ pint passata
2 tablespoons red wine vinegar
6 anchovy fillets, cut in to long strips
50 g/2 oz capers, roughly chopped
125 g/4 oz black olives, pitted
75 g/3 oz pine nuts
handful of flat leaf parsley, chopped
pepper

broccoli with anchovies

75 g/3 oz pine nuts
1 kg/2 lb broccoli, cut
    in to florets
50 g/2 oz butter
juice of 1 lemon
4 anchovy fillets, finely
    chopped
75 g/3 oz Parmesan
    cheese, freshly
    grated
salt and pepper

one   Place the pine nuts under a preheated grill or in a heavy frying pan and dry-fry until golden all over. Set aside.

two   Steam the broccoli or plunge it in to boiling water for 2 minutes, then drain well and transfer to a bowl.

three   Melt the butter in a small saucepan, add the lemon juice and anchovies and heat until the butter foams. Pour the melted butter over the broccoli, sprinkle with salt and pepper and toss. To serve, top the broccoli with the Parmesan and pine nuts.

Preparation time **5 minutes**   Cooking time **20 minutes**
Oven temperature **200°C (400°F), Gas Mark 6**
Total time **25 minutes**   *Serves 4*

potatoes wrapped in Parma ham

one   Roll each potato in a slice of Parma ham, patting with your hands to mould the ham to the shape of the potato.

two   Lightly oil a roasting tin, add the potatoes and cook in a preheated oven, 200°C (400°F), Gas Mark 6, for 20 minutes. Keep an eye on the potatoes while they are cooking as they may need turning, or moving around; often the ones on the edge get more colour than the ones in the middle.

three Serve the potatoes sprinkled with sea salt.

12 small new potatoes,
  cooked
12 very thin slices
  Parma ham
2 tablespoons olive oil
sea salt

Preparation time **5 minutes**   Cooking time **25 minutes**
Oven temperature **230°C (450°F), Gas Mark 8**   Total time **30 minutes**   *Serves 4*

roast potatoes with rosemary and garlic

one   Cut the potatoes lengthways in to quarters, and make sure that they are dry.

two   Put 2 tablespoons of the olive oil in to a large roasting tin, and place in a preheated oven, 230°C (450°F), Gas Mark 8, to warm through.

three Mix together the remaining oil and the rosemary and toss the potatoes to coat them completely.

four   Add the potatoes to the roasting tin in the oven, shake carefully to give an even layer, then place the tin at the top of the oven and roast for 20 minutes.

five   Remove the tin from the oven and move the potatoes around so that they cook evenly. Scatter the garlic amongst the potatoes, return the tin to the oven and cook for a further 5 minutes. Remove the potatoes from the oven, season with salt and pepper and serve immediately.

750 g/1½ lb medium potatoes,
  unpeeled
4 tablespoons olive oil
2 tablespoons chopped rosemary
4 garlic cloves, peeled and sliced
salt and pepper

These potatoes are quite delicious and make an excellent accompaniment to fish, or can be served on their own as a starter. Alternatively, use very small potatoes and serve them with drinks.

Preparation time **5 minutes**   Cooking time **10 minutes**   Total time **15 minutes**   *Serves 4*

cavolo nero with pancetta

1 tablespoon olive oil
1 onion, sliced
1 garlic clove, crushed and chopped
1 red chilli, cored, deseeded and diced
125 g/4 oz pancetta, diced
1 head cavolo nero
75 ml/3 fl oz chicken stock
75 g/3 oz Parmesan cheese, coarsely grated
salt and pepper

one   Heat the olive oil in a large saucepan, add the onion, garlic, chilli and pancetta and sauté for 5 minutes or until soft.

two   To prepare the cavolo nero, trim any wilting leaves then cut the heads in half lengthways. Remove and discard the hard central stem and roughly chop the leaves.

three   Add the cavolo nero to the onion mixture and stir well. Pour in the chicken stock and season with salt and pepper; cook for 4 minutes over a moderate heat, stirring all the time.

four   Finally add the grated Parmesan and serve at once.

Preparation time **5 minutes**   Cooking time **25 minutes**
Total time **30 minutes**   *Serves 4*

braised broad beans and lentils

2 tablespoons olive oil
1 red onion, chopped
2 garlic cloves, crushed and chopped
125 g/4 oz pancetta or unsmoked bacon, diced
175 g/6 oz puy lentils
1 kg/2 lb fresh or frozen broad beans
handful of marjoram, chopped
8 fresh or canned artichoke hearts, prepared
50 g/2 oz butter
handful of flat leaf parsley, chopped
salt and pepper

one   Heat the oil in a heavy-bottomed saucepan, add the onion, garlic and pancetta and sauté for 5 minutes.

two   Add the lentils, broad beans, marjoram, season with salt and pepper and cover with hot water. Mix well and simmer for 15 minutes. The water may need to be topped up during cooking if the mixture is getting too thick and sticking on the bottom of the pan. Keep stirring, just to check that it does not stick.

three   Add the artichoke hearts and cook for 5 minutes. The mixture should be thick and rich. Finally stir in the butter and parsley, taste for seasoning and serve immediately.

Cavolo nero is an Italian cabbage with extremely long leaves, which is available in most of the larger supermarkets. It is almost the shape of a Cos lettuce, but the leaves are greeny purple in colour. Cavolo nero has a simple cabbage-like flavour but a slightly firmer texture. Like all green cabbage it is best not overcooked.

Fish and Shellfish

An abundance of fresh fish and shellfish is available in Italy. Chargrilling and simple cooking are the most popular methods of treating fresh fish.

Preparation time **5 minutes**   Cooking time **7 minutes**
Total time **12 minutes**   *Serves 4*

grilled sea bass

extra virgin olive oil
2 x 1 kg/2 lb sea bass, filleted and halved.
salt and pepper
2 lemons, halved, to serve

one   Lightly oil a baking sheet. Place the 4 sea bass fillets on the baking sheet and drizzle with olive oil. Season generously with salt and pepper and cook under a preheated very hot grill for 7 minutes. Serve with lemon halves and Braised Broad Beans and Lentils (see page 84).

Preparation time **10 minutes**
Cooking time **15 minutes**
Total time **25 minutes**   *Serves 4*

swordfish steaks in white wine and tomatoes

Choose a saucepan that the pieces of fish will fit in to as neatly as possible: a frying pan may be best.

2 tablespoons olive oil
1 red onion, chopped
1 garlic clove, crushed and chopped
2 celery sticks, chopped
2 bay leaves
4 tomatoes, skinned and chopped
1 teaspoon sugar
300 ml/½ pint white wine
2 tablespoons chopped oregano
4 x 175g/6 oz swordfish steaks
salt and pepper

one   Heat the oil in a pan, add the onion, garlic and celery and sauté gently for 5 minutes.

two   Add the bay leaves, tomatoes, sugar, white wine and oregano, season with salt and pepper, mix well and bring to a gentle simmer.

three   Add the swordfish steaks and cook for 5 minutes, then turn them over and cook on the other side for a further 5 minutes. This dish can be served straight away, or in hot weather it is very good at room temperature.

spicy fried sardines

Sardines must be fresh, bright eyed, with shiny fresh scales and without an unpleasant smell. If you have any doubts don't buy them. To gut the sardines, if the fishmonger hasn't done it for you, insert a knife in the belly, make a slit and remove the contents. Cut off the heads just behind the gills and thoroughly wash the fish under cold running water. Drain and dry well.

oil, for deep-frying
125 g/4 oz plain flour
750 g/1½ lb large, fresh sardines
4 tablespoons olive oil
5 shallots, sliced
125 ml/4 fl oz white wine vinegar
4 garlic cloves, crushed and chopped
large handful of mint leaves, finely chopped
rind and juice of 1 lemon
½ teaspoon crushed dried chillies
salt and pepper

one   Heat the oil for deep-frying. Season the flour with salt and pepper.

two   Dip the sardines in to the seasoned flour and fry in the hot oil for 2 minutes or until golden. Remove and place on a tray lined with kitchen paper to absorb the excess oil. Keep warm.

three   Heat 1 tablespoon of the olive oil in a saucepan, add the shallots and sauté for 5 minutes, then add the vinegar and cook until nearly half of it has evaporated.

four   Transfer the sardines to a warmed serving dish. Add the remaining olive oil, the garlic, mint, lemon rind and juice and chillies to the onion mixture and cook for 1 minute. Spoon the sauce over the sardines and sprinkle with salt and pepper. This dish can be served hot or at room temperature.

Preparation time **5 minutes**   Cooking time **15 minutes**   Total time **20 minutes**   *Serves 4*

tuna steaks with sun-dried tomatoes

2 tablespoons olive oil
1 red onion, finely chopped
2 garlic cloves, crushed and chopped
1 rosemary sprig, chopped
75 g/3 oz plain flour
4 x 175 g/6 oz tuna steaks, skinned
oil, for frying
125 g/4 oz sun-dried tomatoes in oil, chopped
75 ml/3 fl oz red wine
1 tablespoon capers
75 g/3 oz black olives
handful of flat leaf parsley, chopped
salt and pepper
1 lemon, cut in to 4 wedges, to serve

one   Heat the olive oil in a saucepan, add the onion, garlic and rosemary and sauté gently for 5 minutes.

two   Season the flour with salt and pepper. Dip the tuna steaks in to the seasoned flour to coat evenly all over.

three   Heat the oil in a frying pan, add the tuna steaks and cook for 4–5 minutes until golden. Turn over and cook on the other side for a further 4–5 minutes. Transfer the tuna steaks to a dish lined with kitchen paper and keep warm in the oven.

four   Add the sun-dried tomatoes to the sautéed onions and stir well. Turn up the heat to high, add the red wine, capers, olives, parsley, season with salt and pepper and simmer for 2 minutes. Serve the sauce with the tuna steaks and wedges of lemon.

Preparation time **10 minutes**
Cooking time **15 minutes**
Total time **25 minutes**
Serves 4

grilled red mullet with salsa verde

4 x 375 g/12 oz red mullet, scaled
and cleaned
Salsa verde:
125 g/4 oz parsley, chopped
125 g/4 oz basil, chopped
5 anchovy fillets, roughly chopped
2 tablespoons capers
2 garlic cloves, crushed and
chopped
juice and rind of 1 lemon
150 ml/¼ pint olive oil
salt and pepper

one Make 3 slashes across the fish on each side and season with salt and pepper. Place under a preheated very hot grill and cook on each side for 6–8 minutes, or until cooked.

two To make the salsa verde, put the parsley, basil, anchovies, capers and garlic in to a food processor or blender and work to a smooth paste. Add the lemon juice and rind and olive oil; season with salt and pepper and blend again.

three Remove the fish from the grill and put a spoonful of the salsa verde in to each of the slashes on one side of the fish. Serve the remaining salsa at the table in a small dish.

trout with Parmesan and basil dressing

Preparation time **10 minutes**
Cooking time **10 minutes**
Total time **20 minutes**
Serves 4

4 tablespoons olive oil
4 x 200 g/7 oz trout fillets
large handful of basil leaves, roughly chopped
1 garlic clove, crushed and chopped
125 g/4 oz Parmesan cheese, freshly grated
salt and pepper

one Lightly brush a baking sheet with oil and place under a preheated very hot grill to heat up.

two Put the trout fillets on to the hot tray, sprinkle with salt and pepper and place under the grill for 5 minutes.

three Put the basil and garlic in to a bowl. Work in the olive oil using a hand-held blender.

four Remove the fish from the grill and sprinkle with the grated Parmesan. Return to the grill and cook for a further 3–5 minutes, until the Parmesan turns golden. Serve with the basil sauce drizzled over the golden trout fillets.

Salsa verde, literally translated as green sauce, is traditionally served with 'bollito mista', a north Italian dish of boiled meats and poultry. It also tastes great on fresh bread.

Preparation time **10 minutes**   Cooking time **15 minutes**   Total time **25 minutes**   *Serves 4*

fish casserole

3 tablespoons olive oil
2 red onions, finely diced
2 garlic cloves, crushed and chopped
½ teaspoon crushed dried chillies
200 g/7 oz squid, cleaned and cut in to thin lengths
200 g/7 oz mussels, scrubbed and debearded
200 g/7 oz clams, cleaned (see page 32)
300 g/10 oz raw tiger prawns in their shells
150 ml/¼ pint fish stock
150 ml/¼ pint dry white wine
½ teaspoon saffron
8 tomatoes, skinned and deseeded
1 bay leaf
1 teaspoon sugar
500 g/1 lb red mullet fillets, cut in to bite-sized pieces
handful of flat leaf parsley, chopped
salt and pepper

one   Heat the oil in a large saucepan – large enough to take all the ingredients. Add the onion and garlic and sauté gently for 5 minutes, then add the chillies and mix well.

two   Add the squid, mussels, clams and tiger prawns and stir well.

three   Add the fish stock, wine, saffron, tomatoes, bay leaf and sugar and season with salt and pepper. Cover the pan and simmer gently for 5 minutes. Discard any mussels or clams that do not open.

four   Add the red mullet, sprinkle with the parsley and simmer for a further 5 minutes, then serve at once. This is a very simple dish to make but finger bowls are needed at the table as it is very messy to eat. Serve with Bruschetta (see page 20) and a green salad.

Preparation time **5 minutes**   Cooking time **25 minutes**
Oven temperature **220°C (425°F), Gas Mark 7**
Total time **30 minutes**   *Serves 4*

baked cod with potatoes and olives

knob of butter
375 g/12 oz potatoes, thinly sliced
thyme sprig, separated in to leaves
4 x 200 g/7 oz cod fillets
2 tablespoons pitted black olives
2 tablespoons olive oil
salt and pepper

one   Rub the butter over a shallow ovenproof dish.

two   Arrange the potatoes in layers in the buttered dish, sprinkling each layer with a little thyme and salt and pepper

three   Place the pieces of cod on top of the potatoes, add the olives, drizzle with olive oil, season with salt and pepper and add a little thyme. Put the dish in the middle of a preheated oven, 220°C (425°F), Gas Mark 7, and cook for 25 minutes. Check that the potatoes are soft before serving.

Preparation time **5 minutes**   Cooking time **25 minutes**   Oven temperature **200°C (400°F), Gas Mark 6**
Total time **30 minutes**   *Serves 4*

halibut in paper parcels

one   Cut 4 sheets of greaseproof paper large enough to enclose the fish and vegetables.

two   To prepare the fennel, trim the top and outer leaves, remove the hard central core and cut the bulb in to slices through the root. Divide evenly among the sheets of greaseproof paper and put the fish on top. Sprinkle with the shallots, olives and sage, season with salt and pepper and finish with a slice of lemon. The greaseproof paper can be folded over and rolled at the edges to seal, but a much easier way is to fold the paper and staple it. Put the parcels on to a baking sheet, and cook in a preheated oven, 200°C (400°F), Gas Mark 6, for 25 minutes.

three Serve these parcels at the table so that everyone opens their own parcel and gets a waft of the delicious aroma that escapes when they are first opened.

1 fennel bulb
4 x 200 g/7 oz halibut fillets
2 shallots, finely chopped
8 pitted black olives
a few sage leaves, torn
4 lemon slices
salt and pepper

Preparation time **10 minutes**   Cooking time **15 minutes**
Oven temperature **220°C (425°F), Gas Mark 7**
Total time **25 minutes**   *Serves 4*

roast monkfish with Parma ham

4 x 175 g/6 oz monkfish fillets
4 rosemary sprigs
8 slices Parma ham
2 tablespoons olive oil
1 red onion, chopped
1 garlic clove, crushed and chopped
6 tomatoes, skinned, deseeded and roughly chopped
1 teaspoon capers, roughly chopped
handful of flat leaf parsley
salt and pepper

one   Season the monkfish with salt and pepper, place the rosemary sprigs on the fish and wrap the slices of Parma ham around them. Put the fish in a lightly oiled baking dish and cook in a preheated oven, 220°C (425°F), Gas Mark 7, for 15 minutes.

two   Heat 1 tablespoon of the oil in a saucepan, add the onion and garlic and sauté gently for 5 minutes.

three Add the tomatoes and capers, mix well then add the remaining olive oil and parsley and season with salt and pepper.

four   Serve the fish with some of the sauce spooned over one end.

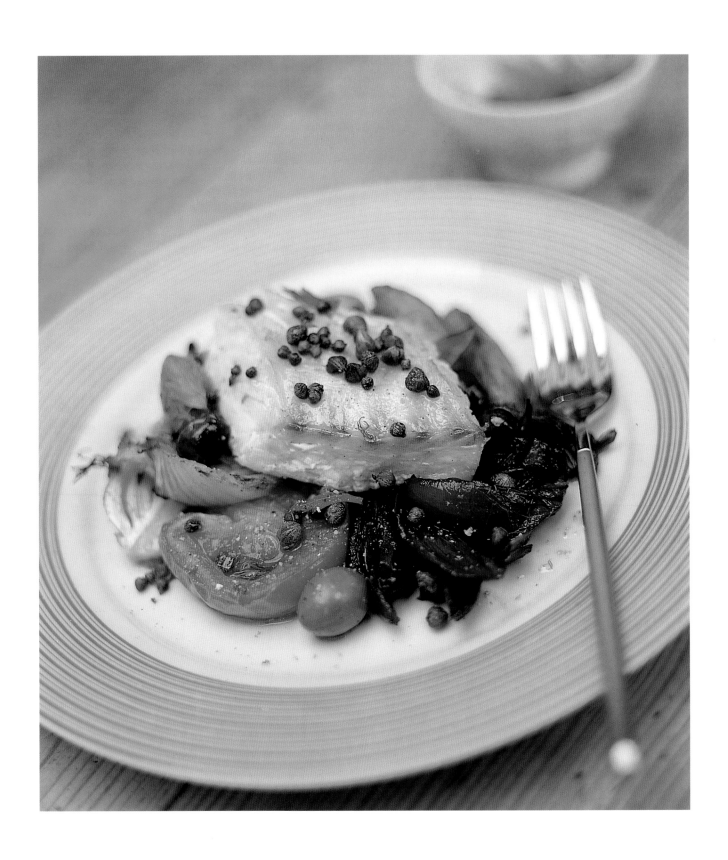

Preparation time **5 minutes**   Cooking time **25 minutes**   Oven temperature 230°C (450°F), Gas Mark 8
Total time **30 minutes**   *Serves 4*

roast cod with vegetables

750 g/1½ lb cod fillets, skinned
4 potatoes, unpeeled and quartered
6 tomatoes, halved
1 red onion, quartered
1 fennel bulb, cut in to wedges
2 garlic cloves, crushed and chopped
75 g/3 oz black olives, pitted
25 g/1 oz green olives, pitted
25 g/1 oz capers
juice of 1 lemon
3 tablespoons olive oil
salt and pepper
handful of parsley, chopped, to garnish

one   Put the cod, potatoes, tomatoes, onion and fennel in to a large lightly oiled dish. Try and arrrange them in a single layer. Sprinkle with the olives, capers and lemon juice and season with salt and pepper.

two   Drizzle with olive oil and place in the top of a preheated oven, 230°C (450°F), Gas Mark 8, and roast for 25 minutes.

three Garnish with flat leaf parsley and serve with warm focaccia bread.

Preparation time **5 minutes**   Cooking time **25 minutes**
Oven temperature **200°C (400°F), Gas Mark 6**   Total time **30 minutes**   *Serves 4*

mussels with fresh tomato and pepper sauce

1 red pepper
2 tablespoons olive oil
2 red onions, chopped
2 garlic cloves, crushed and chopped
6 tomatoes, peeled and chopped
½ teaspoon crushed dried chilli
125 ml/4 fl oz dry white wine
1 kg/2 lb mussels, scrubbed and debearded
2 tablespoons capers
large handful of flat leaf parsley, roughly chopped
salt and pepper

one   To skin the red pepper, first cut off the bottom of the pepper. Put the pepper on the chopping board and slice off 4–5 flat pieces, leaving the seeds and core intact. Place the pepper pieces under a hot grill and leave to blister and blacken, then peel off the skins and roughly chop the flesh.

two   Heat the oil in a large ovenproof casserole, add the onions and garlic and sauté for 5 minutes. Do not brown.

three Add the tomatoes, chilli and white wine and simmer for 5 minutes to reduce and thicken the sauce.

four   Add the mussels and capers and season with salt and pepper. Mix well, cover with a lid and bake in a preheated oven, 200°C (400°F), Gas Mark 6, for 8 minutes.

five   Remove the casserole from the oven. Check the mussels and discard any that have not opened. Stir in the parsley and serve with warm focaccia bread.

Preparation time **15 minutes**   Cooking time **6 minutes**   Total time **21 minutes**   *Serves 4*

pan-fried squid with chillies

1 kg/2 lb small squid, cleaned
2 tablespoons olive oil
3 garlic cloves, crushed and chopped
1 red chilli, finely chopped.
juice of 1 lemon
handful of flat leaf parsley, chopped
salt and pepper

one   Slit the squid down one side and lay them flat. Score the skin of each one with a fine criss-cross pattern.

two   Mix the olive oil, garlic, chilli and lemon juice in a bowl and add the squid. Mix well to coat all over, cover and marinate for 15 minutes.

three   Remove the squid from the marinade, reserving the marinade. Heat a large frying pan or a wok with 2 tablespoons of oil until it is just smoking. Add the squid, season with salt and pepper, stir well and cook over a high heat for 2–3 minutes. The squid will curl up, but just hold them flat for a few seconds to get a tasty browned outside. Finally add the strained marinade and the parsley to the pan, mix well and serve at once.

Preparation time **5 minutes**   Cooking time **6 minutes**   Total time **11 minutes**   *Serves 4*

tiger prawns with garlic and herbs

50 g/2 oz butter
2 tablespoons olive oil
750 g/1½ lb peeled raw tiger prawns
1 shallot, finely diced
2 garlic cloves, crushed and chopped
75 ml/3 fl oz dry white wine
125 g/4 oz flat leaf parsley, chopped
125 g/4 oz marjoram, chopped
salt and pepper

This dish goes very well with egg pasta, or it can be served on its own with warm ciabatta bread to mop up all the juices.

one   Melt the butter with the oil in a frying pan, add the tiger prawns, shallot and garlic and sauté for 5 minutes or until all the prawns have turned pink.

two   Add the white wine, parsley and marjoram and season with salt and pepper. Mix well and serve immediately.

Preparation time **10 minutes**   Cooking time **5 minutes**   Total time **15 minutes**   *Serves 4*

seared scallops with basil and balsamic vinegar

16 large scallops, cleaned
3 tablespoons olive oil
2 shallots, finely chopped
4 tablespoons balsamic vinegar
large handful of basil leaves, torn
salt and pepper

one   Check that the scallops are clean; there should be no wet brown patches. If there are, trim them off leaving the white meat and orange coral.

two   Heat the oil in a large frying pan, over a high heat, until it is just smoking, then add the scallops and cook for 2 minutes on one side. Turn them over and add the shallots. Cook for 1 minute, then reduce the heat. Add the balsamic vinegar and season with salt and pepper, then turn the scallops to coat in the vinegar.

three   Sprinkle the basil over the scallops, quickly mix and serve at once.

Chop the squid tentacles and use them in this dish as they look very pretty. Their faint purple colour is subtly complemented by the red chilli.

Poultry, Game and Meat

High quality meat and game are available throughout Italy, so often all that is needed is brief cooking and a sprinkling of olive oil, salt and black pepper. Older cuts are simmered in rich wine sauces to produce wonderfully tender dishes.

Preparation time **10 minutes** Cooking time **20 minutes**
Total time **30 minutes** *Serves 4*

country chicken

50 g/2 oz butter
2 tablespoons olive oil
4 boneless chicken breasts
1 onion, chopped
½ small celery head, chopped
1 garlic clove, crushed and chopped
½ teaspoon crushed dried chilli
300 ml/½ pint passata
1 bay leaf
thyme sprig
handful of oregano, roughly chopped
salt and pepper

one Melt the butter with the oil in a frying pan. When it is hot, add the chicken breasts and cook on each side for about 5 minutes. Let them brown as this adds to the flavour of the sauce.

two Remove the chicken with a slotted spoon and set aside. Add the onion, celery, garlic and chilli to the pan and sauté for 5 minutes.

three Add the passata, bay leaf and thyme. Season with salt and pepper and stir well. Return the chicken breasts to the sauce and simmer for 10 minutes. Just before serving add the roughly chopped oregano.

Preparation time **5 minutes**
Cooking time **25 minutes**
Total time **30 minutes** *Serves 4*

chicken with wild mushrooms

50 g/2 oz dried wild mushrooms, soaked, or 250 g/8 oz fresh mushrooms, sliced
50 g/ 2 oz plain flour
4 skinless, boneless chicken breasts
50 g/2 oz butter
1 tablespoon olive oil
2 shallots, diced
2 garlic cloves, crushed and chopped
125 ml/4 fl oz white wine
125 g/4 oz mascarpone cheese
handful of chives, snipped
salt and pepper

one If using dried mushrooms, put them in to a bowl and just cover with hot water. Leave to soak for 15 minutes.

two Meanwhile, season the flour with salt and pepper and toss the chicken in the seasoned flour to cover all over.

three Heat the butter and oil in a frying pan, add the chicken and cook on each side for 4 minutes or until coloured. Remove the chicken and keep warm.

four Add the shallots and garlic to the pan and sauté gently for 5 minutes. Add the wine and mix well to include any tasty brown bits from the pan.

five Add the mascarpone and the mushrooms to the pan; if using wild mushrooms, add the soaking liquid. Mix well to melt the mascarpone. If the mixture is very runny, turn up the heat to evaporate some of the liquid. If you are using fresh mushrooms, add a little extra liquid, but mushrooms make their own liquid as they cook.

six Return the chicken to the pan and simmer gently for 10 minutes, turning it from time to time. Finally stir the chives in to the pan and serve immediately.

Preparation time **5 minutes**
Cooking time **25 minutes**
Total time **30 minutes**
Serves 4

Roman chicken

4 tablespoons olive oil
2 red onions, sliced
2 garlic cloves, sliced
2 red peppers, cored, deseeded and sliced
2 yellow peppers, cored, deseeded and sliced
½ teaspoon crushed dried chillies
8 boneless chicken thighs
100 ml/3½ fl oz white wine
large handful of basil, roughly torn
salt and pepper

one Heat the olive oil in a large frying pan, add the onions, garlic, red and yellow peppers and chillies and sauté for 5 minutes.

two Add the chicken thighs, pushing them down to the bottom of the pan to seal on the outside. Cook for a further 5 minutes.

three Add the wine and salt and pepper to taste, cover the pan and cook for about 15 minutes over a low heat. Check occasionally that the chicken and sauce do not stick to the bottom of the pan and add a little more wine, if necessary.

four Stir in the basil just before serving.

Preparation time **5 minutes, plus marinating**   Cooking time **15 minutes**
Total time **25 minutes**   *Serves 4*

chicken with rosemary and garlic

2 tablespoons olive oil
2 tablespoons white wine vinegar
2 tablespoons chopped rosemary
3 garlic cloves, crushed and chopped
1 teaspoon paprika
pared rind of 1 lemon
4 boneless, skinless chicken breasts, cut in to long thin strips
handful of flat leaf parsley, chopped
salt and pepper

one Mix together the olive oil, vinegar, rosemary, garlic, paprika and lemon rind in a bowl and season with salt and pepper. Add the chicken and mix well, then leave to marinate for 10 minutes. Alternatively, this could be done the night before.

two Heat a large nonstick pan, add the chicken and the marinade, mix well and cook over a moderate heat, stirring constantly, for 15 minutes.

three To serve, stir in the chopped parsley.

Preparation time **10 minutes**   Cooking time **20 minutes**
Oven temperature **200°C (400°F), Gas Mark 6**   Total time **30 minutes**   *Serves 4*

black olive chicken rolls

3 garlic cloves, crushed and chopped
2 tablespoons capers
4 anchovy fillets, chopped
1 teaspoon thyme leaves
1 shallot, chopped
175 g/6 oz pitted black olives
1 tablespoon olive oil
4 small boneless, skinless chicken breasts
salt and pepper

one   Put the garlic, capers, anchovies, thyme, shallot, olives and olive oil in to a food processor or blender and whizz together.

two   Place each chicken breast between 2 sheets of greaseproof paper and flatten to about 2½ times its original size by pounding with a rolling pin. Season the chicken breasts with salt and pepper and spread each one with a thin layer of the olive paste.

three   Roll up the breasts and secure with 2 wooden cocktail sticks. Cut each chicken roll in half and place in a lightly oiled ovenproof dish. Cover with foil and cook in the top of a preheated oven, 200°C (400°F), Gas Mark 6, for 20 minutes or until cooked. Serve with pasta tossed in olive oil, parsley and Parmesan.

Preparation time **5 minutes**   Cooking time **25 minutes**
Oven temperature **200°C (400°F), Gas Mark 6**
Total time **30 minutes**   *Serves 4*

chicken stuffed with spinach and ricotta

4 boneless, skinless chicken breasts
125 g/4 oz ricotta cheese
125 g/4 oz cooked spinach, squeezed dry
¼ teaspoon grated nutmeg
8 slices Parma ham
2 tablespoons olive oil
salt and pepper

one   Make a long horizontal slit through the thickness of each chicken breast without cutting right through.

two   Crumble the ricotta in to a bowl. Chop the spinach and add to the ricotta with the nutmeg. Season with salt and pepper and mix well.

three   Divide the stuffing between the 4 chicken breasts and wrap each one in 2 pieces of Parma ham, winding it around the chicken to totally cover the meat.

four   Heat the oil in a shallow ovenproof pan, add the chicken breasts and sauté for 4 minutes on each side or until the ham starts to brown. Transfer the pan to a preheated oven, 200°C (400°F), Gas Mark 6, and cook for 15 minutes. The ham should be browned and slightly crunchy on the outside and the chicken moist and soft.

Preparation time **10 minutes**
Cooking time **20 minutes**
Total time **30 minutes** *Serves 4*

rolled stuffed chicken breasts

4 boneless, skinless chicken breasts
4 slices Parma ham
4 thin slices buffalo mozzarella
4 asparagus tips
75 g/3 oz plain flour
1 tablespoon olive oil
50 g/2 oz butter
50 ml/2 fl oz dry white wine
75 ml/3 fl oz chicken stock
salt and pepper

one   Place each chicken breast between 2 sheets of greaseproof paper and flatten to about 2½ times its original size by pounding with a rolling pin.

two   Season the chicken with salt and pepper, place a slice of Parma ham, a slice of mozzarella and an asparagus tip on top and tightly roll up the chicken escalopes. Tie with a piece of strong thread or spear with wooden cocktail sticks.

three   Season the flour with salt and pepper. Dip the prepared chicken rolls in the flour, coating them evenly all over.

four   Heat the olive oil and half of the butter in a frying pan, add the chicken rolls and sauté over a low heat for 15 minutes or until golden all over, turning frequently to brown the chicken evenly.

five   Remove the chicken, place in a warmed serving dish and keep warm. Pour the wine and chicken stock in to the pan, bring to the boil and simmer for 3 minutes.

six   Remove the thread or cocktail sticks just before serving the chicken. Add the remaining butter to the pan, mix quickly with a small whisk to emulsify the sauce, then spoon over the chicken and serve with steamed asparagus.

Preparation time **5 minutes**
Cooking time **10 minutes**
Total time **15 minutes** *Serves 4*

chicken livers with Marsala and oregano

75 g/3 oz butter
50 g/2 oz pancetta or bacon, diced
1 shallot, diced
1 garlic clove, crushed and chopped
500 g/1 lb chicken livers, trimmed
175 ml/6 fl oz Marsala
1 tablespoon chopped oregano
salt and pepper

one   Melt half of the butter in a large frying pan, add the pancetta, shallot and garlic and sauté for 5 minutes without allowing to colour, then remove from the pan.

two   Melt the remaining butter, add the chicken livers and cook over a high heat for 3 minutes until the chicken livers are evenly brown on the outside. Chicken livers are best when browned on the outside but still pink in the middle.

three   Return the shallot mixture to the pan and mix well. Add the Marsala and oregano and season with salt and pepper. Bring quickly to the boil. Serve immediately with buttered tagliatelle.

Preparation time **5 minutes**   Cooking time **25 minutes**   Total time **30 minutes**   *Serves 4*

duck breasts with balsamic vinegar

one   Heat the oil in a frying pan, add the duck breasts, skin side down, and cook over a moderate heat for 5 minutes, then reduce the heat and cook for another 10 minutes. Drain the excess oil from the duck skin.

two   Turn the duck breasts over and add the balsamic vinegar along with the cranberries and sugar. Season with salt and pepper and cook for a further 10 minutes.

three   Serve the duck breast with the sauce spooned over. The cranberries will have broken down and made a delicious sauce with the vinegar and duck juices, and the duck breasts should be pink and juicy in the middle.

1 tablespoon oil
4 boneless duck breasts
4 tablespoons balsamic vinegar
75 g/3 oz cranberries
50 g/2 oz brown sugar
salt and pepper

Preparation time **10 minutes**   Cooking time **20 minutes**
Total time **30 minutes**   *Serves 4*

grilled guinea fowl with fresh herb sauce

4 boneless guinea fowl breasts
2 tablespoons olive oil
salt and pepper
Herb sauce:
3 garlic cloves, crushed and chopped
4 anchovy fillets, chopped
large handful of flat leaf parsley
handful of rocket leaves
handful of sorrel leaves
handful of basil leaves
juice of ½ lemon
125 ml/4 fl oz extra virgin olive oil

one   Put the guinea fowl breasts, skin side up, on a lightly oiled grill pan, brush with a little olive oil and season with salt and pepper. Place the pan under a preheated hot grill and cook the guinea fowl for about 10 minutes on each side.

two   Meanwhile, make the herb sauce. Put the garlic, anchovies, parsley, rocket, sorrel, basil and lemon juice in a food processor or blender and whizz for 1 minute. With the motor running, slowly drizzle in the olive oil; the sauce should be thick and bright green with a strong fresh aroma. Finally season with salt and pepper and blend again.

three   The guinea fowl is ready when the skin is crunchy and dark brown. Serve with a little herb sauce on each plate and the rest at the table in a small dish.

This herb sauce is best eaten the day it is made but can be kept for 1 day; it just loses its fresh aroma and bright green colour.

braised breast of wood pigeon

75 g/3 oz plain flour
8 wood pigeon breasts, skinned
2 tablespoons olive oil
1 red onion, chopped
2 garlic cloves, crushed and chopped
3 celery sticks, chopped
250 ml/8 fl oz red wine
grated rind of 1 orange
thyme sprig
rosemary sprig
1 bay leaf
½ teaspoon ground cinnamon
2 teaspoons juniper berries, crushed
200 g/7 oz redcurrant jelly
handful of flat leaf parsley, chopped
salt and pepper

one   Season the flour with salt and pepper. Dip the wood pigeon breasts in to the seasoned flour and coat evenly.

two   Heat the oil in a wide saucepan, add the pigeon breasts and cook for 2 minutes on each side. Remove from the pan.

three Add the onion, garlic and celery and sauté for 5 minutes. Increase the heat and pour in the red wine, stirring well to incorporate any tasty brown bits from the pan.

four   Add the orange rind, thyme, rosemary, bay leaf, cinnamon, juniper berries, redcurrant jelly and season with salt and pepper. Return the pigeon breasts to the pan and baste well with the sauce. Simmer for 10 minutes.

five   Remove the pigeon from the pan and keep warm. Increase the heat and reduce the liquid to make a rich glaze for the pigeon. Return the pigeon breasts to the pan, add the parsley and serve.

quail with artichoke hearts

75 g/3 oz plain flour
4 prepared quails, weighing 250 g/8 oz each
2 tablespoons olive oil
1 onion, chopped
2 celery sticks, chopped
2 garlic cloves, peeled and crushed
300 ml/½ pint white wine
handful of sage, chopped
400 g/13 oz jar prepared artichoke hearts
salt and pepper

one   Sprinkle the flour on a plate and season with salt and pepper. Dip the quail in the seasoned flour, coating them evenly.

two   Heat the oil in a large saucepan, add the quail and brown all over. Remove from the pan and keep warm.

three Add the onion, celery and garlic and sauté for 3 minutes, then pour in the wine scraping any browned bits from the bottom of the pan.

four   Return the quail to the pan with the sage and artichoke hearts and season well. Cover the pan and simmer for 20 minutes, turning the quail from time to time. Serve with fresh pasta tossed in butter.

This dish is very good made the night before and left for all the flavours to mingle. When buying the quails ask the butcher to take off the skin, cut the quails in half and remove the spine from each bird.

Serve the rabbit on a bed of pappardelle, if liked. Pappardelle is the traditional pasta to be served with game.

Preparation time **5 minutes**   Cooking time **25 minutes**
Total time **30 minutes**   *Serves 4*

pan cooked
rabbit with sage

2 tablespoons olive oil
1 rabbit, cut in to 8 pieces
handful of chopped sage
1 large rosemary sprig
150 ml/¼ pint dry white wine
1 tablespoon Dijon mustard
salt and pepper
handful of flat leaf parsley,
chopped, to serve

one   Heat the oil in a large frying pan, add the rabbit pieces and brown all over.

two   Season well with salt and pepper. Add the sage, rosemary, wine and mustard, mix thoroughly and coat the rabbit in the wine sauce.

three   Simmer the rabbit for 20 minutes, turning frequently so that it cooks evenly.

four   To serve, sprinkle the rabbit pieces generously with the roughly chopped parsley.

Preparation time **5 minutes**   Cooking time **25 minutes**
Total time **30 minutes**   *Serves 4*

sweet and
sour rabbit

75 g/3 oz plain flour
1 rabbit, cut in to 8 pieces
2 tablespoons olive oil
1 onion, diced
1 garlic clove, crushed and chopped
300 ml/½ pint red wine
rosemary sprig
4 tablespoons balsamic vinegar
1 tablespoon brown sugar
2 tablespoons sultanas
2 tablespoons pine nuts, toasted
2 tablespoons black olives, pitted and
roughly chopped
salt and pepper

one   Season the flour with the salt and pepper. Coat the rabbit evenly all over in the seasoned flour.

two   Heat the olive oil in a large frying pan, add the rabbit pieces, turning to brown them all over, then remove with a slotted spoon and set aside.

three   Add the onion and garlic and sauté for 5 minutes; do not brown, just soften.

four   Return the rabbit to the pan, pour in the red wine, and add the rosemary, vinegar, sugar, sultanas and season with salt and pepper. Simmer.for 20 minutes, turning the rabbit to coat it in the sauce and cook evenly.

five   Just before serving add the pine nuts and olives and stir to mix well.

Preparation time **10 minutes**
Cooking time **15 minutes**
Total time **25 minutes**   *Serves 4*

Preparation time **5 minutes**   Cooking time **25 minutes**
Oven temperature **230°C (450°F), Gas Mark 8**
Total time **30 minutes**   *Serves 4*

grilled fillet of venison

roast pork fillet with rosemary and fennel

4 x 175 g/6 oz venison fillet steaks
2 tablespoons olive oil
1 shallot, finely chopped
2 garlic cloves, crushed and chopped
250 ml/8 fl oz red wine
4 cloves
1 piece cinnamon stick
pared rind of 1 orange
10 juniper berries, crushed
3 tablespoons redcurrant jelly
salt and pepper

1 large rosemary sprig
3 garlic cloves
750 g/1½ lb pork fillet, trimmed
4 tablespoons olive oil
2 fennel bulbs, trimmed and cut in to wedges, central core removed
150 ml/¼ pint white wine
75 g/3 oz mascarpone cheese
salt and pepper
rosemary sprigs, to garnish

one   Brush the venison steaks with the olive oil and season well with salt and pepper.

two   Heat a little oil in a saucepan, add the shallot and garlic and sauté for 3 minutes. Add the wine, cloves, cinnamon, orange rind, juniper berries and redcurrant jelly and simmer until it reduces to a rich sauce.

three While the sauce is cooking, place the venison fillets on a grill rack and cook under a preheated hot grill for 6 minutes on each side.

four   To serve, strain the sauce and spoon over the venison steaks. Serve with pasta tossed in butter or Creamed Polenta with Dolcelatte and Mascarpone (see page 54).

one   Break the rosemary in to short pieces and cut the garlic in to slices. Pierce the pork with a sharp knife and inset the pieces of rosemary and garlic evenly all over the fillet.

two   Heat 2 tablespoons of the olive oil in a frying pan, add the pork fillet and fry for 5 minutes or until browned all over.

three Lightly oil a roasting tin, add the fennel and drizzle with olive oil. Place the pork fillet on top, season generously and roast in a preheated oven, 230°C (450°F), Gas Mark 8, for 20 minutes.

four   Pour the wine in to the frying pan and simmer until reduced by half. Add the mascarpone and season with salt and pepper. Stir to mix well.

five   To serve, cut the pork in to slices and arrange on a warmed serving dish with wedges of fennel. Pour the sauce in to the roasting pan and place on the heat. Using a wooden spoon stir all the tasty bits in to the sauce then spoon over the pork and fennel. Garnish with rosemary.

Preparation time **5 minutes, plus marinating**
Cooking time **10 minutes**   Total time **15 minutes**   *Serves 4*

lamb chops with rosemary and lemon

1 rosemary sprig, finely chopped
1 tablespoon olive oil
rind and juice of 1 lemon
8 lamb cutlets
salt and pepper

It is important that the grill is very hot for this recipe. It seals the meat quickly and browns the outside, leaving the inside pink.

one   Mix the rosemary, olive oil and lemon rind and juice in a shallow dish and season with salt and pepper. Add the lamb cutlets and coat with the marinade. Leave to marinate for 10 minutes.

two   Place the chops on a grill pan and spoon over the marinade. Place under a preheated very hot grill and cook for 5 minutes on each side. Serve with Creamed Polenta with Dolcelatte and Mascarpone (see page 54).

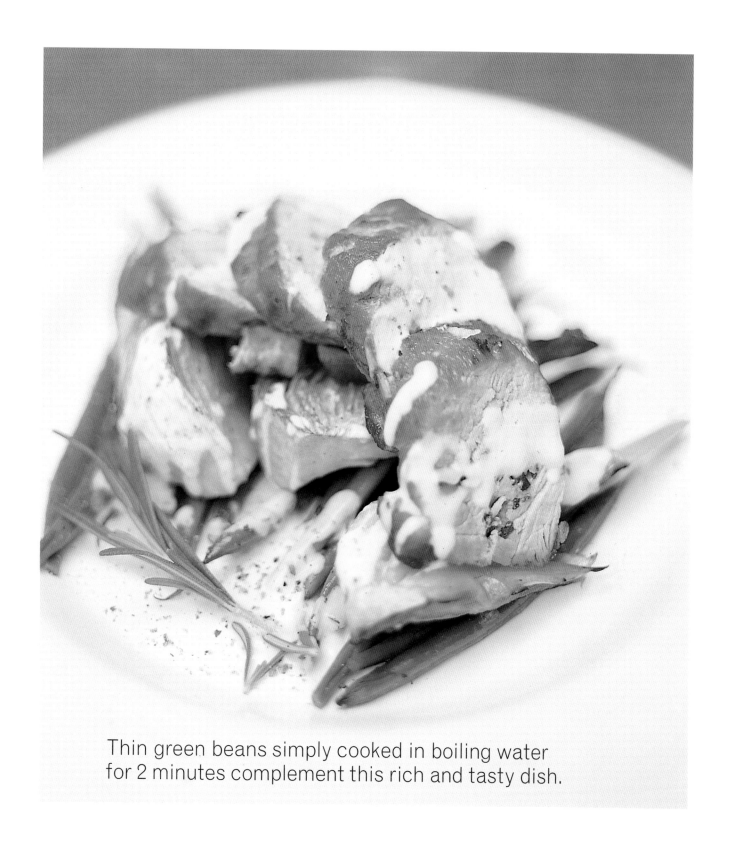

Thin green beans simply cooked in boiling water
for 2 minutes complement this rich and tasty dish.

Preparation time **10 minutes**   Cooking time **10 minutes**   Total time **20 minutes**   *Serves 4*

Parmesan breaded lamb chops

75 g/3 oz plain flour
8 lamb chops, trimmed
50 g/2 oz Parmesan cheese, freshly grated
50 g/2 oz fresh breadcrumbs
2 eggs, beaten
2 tablespoons olive oil
salt and pepper
1 lemon, cut in to 4 wedges, to serve

one   Season the flour with salt and pepper. Dip the lamb chops in to the seasoned flour, coating them evenly all over. Mix together the Parmesan and breadcrumbs and season with salt and pepper.

two   Dip the cutlets first in the beaten egg and then in to the Parmesan mixture and coat all over, pressing the crumbs on to the lamb.

three   Heat the oil in a frying pan, add the lamb chops and cook on each side for 4 minutes or until golden. Take care when turning them over; a palette knife is best, so as not to loosen any of the cheesy crust from the chops.

four   Serve immediately with lemon wedges.

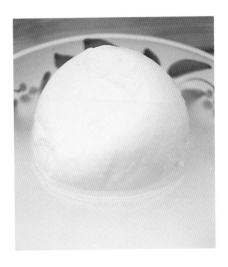

Preparation time **10 minutes**   Cooking time **8 minutes**   Total time **18 minutes**   *Serves 4*

fillet steak wrapped in Parma ham

handful of chopped marjoram
2 garlic cloves, crushed and finely chopped
4 x 175 g/6 oz fillet steaks
8 slices Parma ham
125 g/4 oz buffalo mozzarella, cut in to 4 slices
salt and pepper

one   Mix together the marjoram and garlic and season with salt and pepper. Coat the steaks with the herb mixture then wrap them in the Parma ham. Make sure that all the steak is covered with the ham.

two   Put the steaks on a greased grill rack and place under a preheated very hot grill, as close to the heat as possible without burning them. Cook on each side for 3 minutes if you like your steak rare, 5–6 minutes for medium and 8 minutes for well done.

three   Place the slices of mozzarella on the steaks, return to the grill and cook until the mozzarella is melting and just turning golden.

four   Remove the steaks from the grill and leave to rest for 5 minutes before serving. This allows the meat to relax.

Preparation time **10 minutes**   Cooking time **10 minutes**   Total time **20 minutes**   *Serves 4*

breaded veal escalopes with Parma ham and Parmesan

one   Place the veal escalopes between 2 sheets of greaseproof paper and flatten them by pounding with a rolling pin or meat mallet.

two   Season the flour with salt and pepper. Dip the escalopes first in the flour, then in the egg and finally in the breadcrumbs, coating them evenly.

three   Melt the butter in a large frying pan. When it is foaming add the escalopes and cook on each side for 1–2 minutes or until golden.

four   Place the escalopes on a grill pan. Put a piece of Parma ham on each one and sprinkle with grated Parmesan. Place the escalopes under a preheated very hot grill and cook for 4–5 minutes until the Parmesan is golden.

five   Garnish the escalopes with chopped parsley and serve with lemon wedges.

4 x 175 g/6 oz veal escalopes
75 g/3 oz plain flour
2 eggs, beaten
175 g/6 oz fresh breadcrumbs
75 g/3 oz butter
50 g/2 oz Parma ham
50 g/2 oz Parmesan cheese, freshly grated
salt and pepper
handful of flat leaf parsley, chopped, to garnish
1 lemon, cut in to 4 wedges, to serve

Preparation time **10 minutes**
Cooking time **10 minutes**
Total time **20 minutes**
Serves 4

veal escalopes with lemon and pine nuts

75 g/3 oz plain flour
4 x 175 g/6 oz veal escalopes
50 g/2 oz butter
1 tablespoon olive oil
75 g/3 oz pine nuts
rind and juice of 1 lemon
75 ml/3 fl oz chicken stock
handful of parsley, finely chopped
salt and pepper

one   Season the flour with salt and pepper. Dip the escalopes in to the seasoned flour, coating them evenly all over.

two   Heat the butter and oil in a frying pan. When it is foaming, add the escalopes and cook on each side for about 3 minutes until golden.

three   Sprinkle the pine nuts in to the pan and stir until golden.

four   Add the lemon rind and juice, chicken stock and parsley and season with salt and pepper. Bring to the boil and mix well. Serve immediately with Risotto alla Milanese (see page 40).

It is important that all the ingredients for the gremolata are finely chopped or grated as they mix together better, making a more subtle blend.

Preparation time **5 minutes**   Cooking time **25 minutes**
Oven temperature **200°C (400°F), Gas Mark 6**   Total time **30 minutes**   *Serves 4*

veal chops with gremolata

4 thin veal chops
75 g/3 oz seasoned flour
50 g/2 oz butter
1 tablespoon olive oil
2 onions, chopped
2 garlic cloves, crushed and chopped
2 celery sticks, chopped
1 carrot, chopped
2 bay leaves
6 tomatoes, skinned, deseeded and chopped
125 ml/4 fl oz chicken stock
125 ml/4 fl oz dry white wine
salt and pepper
Gremolata:
2 tablespoons finely chopped parsley
1 tablespoon finely chopped sage
rind of 3 lemons, finely grated
3 large garlic cloves, crushed and chopped

one   Coat both sides of the veal chops with seasoned flour. Melt the butter and oil in a flameproof casserole, add the chops and brown well on each side. Remove from the casserole and keep warm.

two   Add the onions, garlic, celery and carrot to the pan and sauté for 3 minutes.

three   Add the bay leaves, tomatoes, stock, wine and salt and pepper, mix well and bring to the boil. Return the chops to the casserole and turn to coat them in the sauce. Cover and cook in a preheated oven, 200°C (400°F), Gas Mark 6, for 20 minutes.

four   While the chops are cooking, make the gremolata. Mix together the parsley, sage, lemon rind and garlic.

five   To serve, transfer the chops to a warmed serving plate and keep them warm. Boil the sauce to reduce if necessary, then pour it over the chops and spoon some of the gremolata over each one.

Preparation time **10 minutes**   Cooking time **15 minutes**
Total time **25 minutes**   *Serves 4*

Venetian calves' liver

one   Heat half of the butter and half of the oil in a large frying pan, add the onions and sauté for 10 minutes. Do not allow to brown. Remove the onions and set aside.

two   Season the liver on both sides with salt and pepper.

three   Add the remaining oil and butter to the pan. When it is foaming, add the liver and cook on a high heat for 2 minutes on each side, or longer if you do not like your liver pink in the middle. Remove the liver and place on a warmed serving plate.

four   Allow the frying pan to heat for a few seconds, then add the wine and return the onions to the pan. Boil rapidly to reduce for 1 minute, then stir in the parsley and pour the sauce over the liver. Serve immediately.

50 g/2 oz butter
2 tablespoons olive oil
2 onions, finely sliced
4 x 175 g/6 oz pieces thinly sliced calves' liver
125 ml/4 fl oz red wine
1 tablespoon finely chopped parsley
salt and pepper

Desserts

This chapter includes
some classic Italian
desserts as well as some
unusual new ideas
including sweet and
chocolate risottos.

Preparation time **15 minutes, plus chilling**   Total time **15 minutes**   *Serves 4*

tiramisu with raspberry surprise

4 tablespoons very strong espresso coffee
2 tablespoons grappa or brandy
10 sponge fingers
125 g/4 oz raspberries
175 g/6 oz mascarpone cheese
2 eggs, separated
50 g/2 oz icing sugar
25 g/1 oz dark chocolate

This dish is best made the night before so that it can set completely.

one   Combine the coffee and grappa or brandy. Dip the sponge fingers in to the liquid to coat them evenly, then arrange them on a small shallow dish or a serving platter, pouring over any excess liquid. Sprinkle the raspberries evenly over the soaked sponge fingers.

two   In a bowl, whisk together the mascarpone, egg yolks and icing sugar until smooth and well blended.

three In another bowl, whisk the egg whites until stiff and glossy, then fold together the egg whites and the mascarpone mixture until well blended.

four   Spoon the mixture over the sponge fingers and smooth the surface. Finely grate the chocolate straight on to the mixture. Cover and chill until set.

Preparation time **5 minutes**
Cooking time **10 minutes**
Total time **15 minutes**   *Serves 4*

zabaglione

4 egg yolks
75 g/3 oz caster sugar, plus extra for
    frosting the glasses
grated rind of ½ lemon
½ teaspoon ground cinnamon, plus extra
    to decorate
1 drop vanilla extract
150 ml/¼ pint Marsala
125 g/4 oz fruit (such as peaches,
    apricots, berries), sliced

one   Place the egg yolks, caster sugar, lemon rind, cinnamon and vanilla extract in a heatproof bowl and beat with an electric whisk until thick, pale and creamy.

two   Place the bowl over a saucepan of simmering water and continue whisking. Slowly add the Marsala and whisk until the mixture is warm, frothy and thick.

three To serve, dip the rims of 4 glasses in water, then in sugar to frost them. Divide the fruit among the glasses, then spoon in the zabaglione. To serve, dust with a little extra cinnamon.

Italian trifle

one   Spread the sponge fingers with the jam and arrange in a glass serving bowl. Sprinkle over the Marsala or sherry and add half of the blueberries.

two   Mix a little milk with the cornflour to make a smooth paste. Stir the paste in to the rest of the milk. Pour in to a saucepan and bring to the boil, stirring all the time as the milk will thicken; when it is boiling and smooth remove it from the heat.

three   Whisk the egg yolks and sugar in a large bowl until they are light and creamy. Add the thickened milk to the beaten egg mixture, whisking all the time. Blend well and pour over the blueberries, then top with the remaining blueberries. Allow to cool.

four   Softly whip the cream and spread over the trifle, then top with the grated chocolate.

This dessert is very good if made the night before to allow all the flavours to blend together.

8 sponge fingers
2 tablespoons blueberry jam
50 ml/2 fl oz Marsala or sherry
250 g/8 oz blueberries
300 ml/½ pint milk
1 tablespoon cornflour
2 egg yolks
2 tablespoons sugar
300 ml/½ pint whipping cream
50 g/2 oz chocolate, grated

blood orange granita

one   Using a sharp knife, cut off the top and bottom of the oranges, then cut away the pith and peel. Working over a bowl to catch the juice, cut the segments out of the oranges and squeeze any excess juice from each one.

two   Strain the juice in a saucepan, add the sugar and heat until it has dissolved.

three   Place the orange flesh in a food processor or blender and whizz until smooth. Mix in the juice and pour in to ice cube trays to freeze.

four   When you serve the granita, first chill the serving dishes for a short while in the freezer. To serve, remove the granita ice cubes from the freezer, put them in the food processor or blender and whizz for 30 seconds, then transfer them to the serving dishes and serve immediately.

1 kg/2 lb blood oranges
250 g/8 oz sugar

Preparation time **5 minutes**   Cooking time **25 minutes**
Oven temperature **180°C (350°F), Gas Mark 4**   Total time **30 minutes**   *Serves 4*

panettone pudding

50 g/2 oz butter
5 slices panettone
a little apricot jam for
spreading
250 ml/8 fl oz milk
250 ml/8 fl oz double
cream
2 eggs
1 egg yolk
50 g/2 oz brown sugar,
plus extra for the crust

one   Butter a 1.2 litre/2 pint ovenproof dish. Spread the panettone slices with the apricot jam and cut them in to triangles or rectangles. Place in the buttered dish; try and arrange them in overlapping layers.

two   Put the milk and cream in to a saucepan and bring gently to the boil.

three   Whisk together the eggs, egg yolk and sugar in a bowl until creamy and fluffy. Continue whisking and slowly add the hot milk and cream. When it is all combined, carefully pour it over the panettone; make sure that it is all covered by the custard mixture. Sprinkle with a little extra sugar to make a nice crunchy crust.

four   Fill a roasting tin with boiling water, place the panettone pudding in the bain marie and bake in a preheated oven, 180°C (350°F), Gas Mark 4, for 25 minutes or until the custard is set.

Preparation time **10 minutes**
Cooking time **10 minutes**
Total time **20 minutes**
Serves 4

caramelized orange and pineapple

4 oranges
175 g/6 oz sugar
125 ml/4 fl oz water
1 small pineapple

one   With a very sharp knife, remove the rind from 2 of the oranges and slice it in to very fine strips. Place the rind in a pan of boiling water and simmer for 2 minutes. Remove and drain well.

two   Put the sugar and water in to a saucepan and heat gently, swishing the pan constantly until the sugar is dissolved. Increase the heat and boil the syrup until it turns a golden brown. Take care not to overcook the caramel as it continues to cook in the pan once it is golden as it has reached such a high temperature. If it does get too dark, carefully add 2 tablespoons of water. Stand back when adding the water as the caramel spits. When it is golden, place it to one side ready to pour over the fruit.

three   To peel the oranges, cut a slice off the top and bottom of each one, then place the orange on one of these cut sides and take a knife around the side of the orange, cutting away the skin and pith. Cut across the orange in to about 6–7 slices.

four   To prepare the pineapple, top and tail it and slice away the skin from top to bottom. Make sure that you remove the 'eyes' close to the skin. Cut the pineapple in to quarters and remove the core. Cut in to slices.

five   Make alternate layers of orange and pineapple in a heatproof dish, sprinkle with the orange rind, pour over the caramel and leave to stand until required.

This dish is very good if prepared up to the cooking stage the night before and then kept in the refrigerator. This allows the panettone to soak up the custard.

Preparation time **5 minutes**   Cooking time **25 minutes**
Oven temperature **180°C (350°F), Gas Mark 4**   Total time **30 minutes**   *Serves 4–6*

lemon polenta syrup cake

175 g/6 oz butter
175 g/6 oz caster sugar
125 g/4 oz ground almonds
50 g/2 oz flaked almonds
½ teaspoon vanilla extract
2 large eggs
finely grated rind and juice of
1 lemon
75 g/3 oz polenta flour
½ teaspoon baking powder
single cream, to serve
Syrup:
grated rind and juice of 2 lemons
50 g/2 oz caster sugar
2 tablespoons of water

one   Line a 15 cm/6 inch cake tin with baking parchment.

two   Beat together the butter and sugar until light and creamy. Add the ground and flaked almonds, vanilla extract and eggs and mix well. Add the lemon rind and juice, polenta and baking powder and mix well. Spoon in to the prepared tin and bake in a preheated oven, 180°C (350°F), Gas Mark 4, for 25 minutes.

three   While the cake is cooking, make the syrup. Put the lemon rind and juice, caster sugar and water in a saucepan and heat through. Spoon over the cake as soon as it comes out of the oven. Allow the syrup to drizzle through. Serve the cake hot or cold with single cream.

Preparation time **10 minutes**   Cooking time **12 minutes**
Oven temperature **220°C (425°F), Gas Mark 7**
Total time **22 minutes**   *Serves 4*

almond soufflés

15 g/½ oz butter, plus extra for
greasing
25 g/1 oz plain flour, plus extra
for dusting
200 ml/7 fl oz milk
75 g/3 oz ground almonds
3 eggs, separated
25 g/1 oz caster sugar
75 ml/3 fl oz Amaretto di Saronno
4 macaroons, crushed
icing sugar, to serve

one   Butter 4 small soufflé dishes and dust with flour.

two   Melt the butter in a small saucepan, add the flour and stir to a smooth paste. Slowly pour in the milk, stirring constantly, to make a smooth sauce. Add the ground almonds and egg yolks; mix well and rapidly. Do not leave the pan on the heat. Add the sugar and Amaretto and mix well.

three   Quickly whisk the egg whites until stiff. Fold in the almond sauce, then quickly fold in the crushed macaroons.

four   Divide the mixture between the prepared soufflé dishes and cook in a preheated oven, 220°C (425°F), Gas Mark 7, for about 12 minutes until risen and golden. Dust with icing sugar and serve immediately.

Preparation time **5 minutes**   Cooking time **15 minutes**
Oven temperature **200°C (400°F), Gas Mark 6**   Total time **20 minutes**   *Serves 4*

baked peaches with almonds and honey

50 g/2 oz butter, plus extra for the dish
4 large ripe peaches, halved and stones removed
50 g/2 oz flaked almonds
4 tablespoons clear honey
a little ground cinnamon
crème fraîche, to serve

one   Butter a shallow baking dish, large enough to take
8 peach halves.

two   Place the peaches in the baking dish, skin side down.
Dot with butter, sprinkle with the almonds, drizzle with the honey
and dust with cinnamon.

three   Bake the peaches at the top of a preheated oven, 200°C
(400°F), Gas Mark 6, for 10–15 minutes. You want to get a little
colour in to the peaches and get the almonds lightly browned.

four   Serve the peaches with the juices drizzled over and
topped with a spoonful of crème fraîche.

Preparation time **5 minutes**   Cooking time **20 minutes**   Total time **25 minutes**   *Serves 4*

poached pears with honey and cinnamon

rind and juice of 1 lemon
450 ml/¾ pint red wine
150 ml/5 fl oz water
5 tablespoons clear honey
1 mace blade
1 cinnamon stick
6 cloves
4 ripe pears, peeled
thick yogurt, to serve

one   Put the lemon rind and juice, red wine,
water, honey, mace, cinnamon and cloves in to a
saucepan and bring to a gentle boil.

two   Add the pears and simmer for 10 minutes,
or until they are soft, turning them occasionally.

three   Remove the pears with a slotted spoon
and set aside. Transfer the liquid to a saucepan
with a larger surface area. Place the pan on a high
heat and boil rapidly to make a rich, thick, sticky
syrup. Spoon the liquid over the pears and serve
with thick yogurt.

Preparation time **10 minutes**   Cooking time **15 minutes**
Oven temperature **180°C (350°F), Gas Mark 4**
Total time **25 minutes**   *Makes approximately 16*

almond macaroons

These macaroons are delicious served with coffee. They can be stored in an airtight container for up to 10 days.

125 g/4 oz ground almonds
150 g/5 oz caster sugar
2 large egg whites
½ teaspoon almond extract

one   Line 3 baking sheets with baking parchment.

two   Mix the ground almonds and sugar thoroughly. Whisk the egg whites and almond extract until stiff and glossy. Add the ground almond mixture to the egg whites and fold in until evenly blended.

three Using a small teaspoon, place spoonfuls of the mixture on the baking sheets leaving space between them so they can expand slightly. Place the baking sheets in a preheated oven, 180°C (350°F), Gas Mark 4, and bake for 15 minutes. The macaroons should be golden and slightly firm.

four   Remove the macaroons from the oven and leave for 5 minutes to cool and set. Lift them off the baking parchment with a thin palette knife and leave to cool completely.

Preparation time **5 minutes**
Cooking time **10 minutes**
Total time **15 minutes**   *Serves 8*

almond brittle

Serve this almond brittle with ice cream or good strong coffee. Store it in an airtight container.

250 g/8 oz blanched almonds
250 g/8 oz sugar

one   Line a baking sheet with baking parchment.

two   Put the almonds on a grill pan and place under a preheated grill until lightly brown. Allow to cool a little, then chop roughly.

three Heat a non-stick frying pan over a moderate heat, add the sugar and allow to melt in to caramel. Take care that the heat is not too high or the caramel will burn and have a very bitter taste. Add the almonds and mix in, then pour the almond brittle in to the prepared baking tray.

four   Leave the almond brittle to cool, then break it in to small pieces.

Serve the chocolate risotto in coffee cups for an Italian flavour. Use a good quality dark chocolate with a high percentage of cocoa butter – at least 70%.

Preparation time **5 minutes**   Cooking time **20 minutes**
Total time **25 minutes**   *Serves 4*

chocolate risotto

one   Put the milk and sugar in to a saucepan and heat to simmering point.

two   Melt the butter in a heavy-bottomed saucepan, add the rice and stir well to coat the grains.

three   Add a ladleful of hot milk and stir well. When the rice has absorbed the milk, add another ladleful. Continue to stir and add the milk until it is all absorbed. The rice should be slightly al dente and with a creamy sauce.

four   Finally add the hazelnuts, sultanas and grated chocolate and mix quickly. Serve decorated with a little grated chocolate. Try not to over-mix the chocolate as the marbled effect looks good. For a special treat add a splash of brandy just before serving. Decorate with grated chocolate.

600 ml/1 pint milk
25 g/1 oz sugar
50 g/2 oz butter
125 g/4 oz arborio or carnaroli rice
50 g/2 oz hazelnuts, toasted and chopped
50 g/2 oz sultanas
125 g/4 oz good quality dark chocolate, grated
splash of brandy (optional)
grated chocolate, to decorate

Preparation time **5 minutes**   Cooking time **20 minutes**   Total time **25 minutes**   *Serves 4*

sweet risotto

This unusual sweet risotto is not unlike a creamy rice pudding, but with more flavour.

600 ml/1 pint milk
25 g/1 oz sugar
½ teaspoon vanilla extract
50 g/2 oz butter
finely grated rind of 1 lemon
125 g/4 oz arborio or carnaroli rice
50 g/2 oz raisins
50 g/2 oz toasted flaked almonds
3 tablespoons honey

one   Put the milk, sugar and vanilla extract in to a saucepan and heat to simmering point, then turn off the heat.

two   Melt the butter in a heavy-bottomed saucepan, add the lemon rind and rice and mix well to coat the grains.

three   Add the raisins and a ladleful of hot milk and stir well. When the rice has absorbed the milk, add another ladleful. Continue to stir and keep adding the milk until it is all absorbed. The rice should be slightly al dente and with a creamy sauce.

four   Serve in individual dishes, sprinkled with toasted almonds and drizzled with honey.

Index

Author's acknowledgments

I really want to say a big thank you to all the people I have worked with: I believe that we all learn from
each other and become inspired, thus new creations evolve. I have worked with chefs both fantastic and
not so fantastic; they all helped as they made me think and influenced my direction. When we are young
it is all about direction and choice, and I am happy with the choices I made as I decided to travel and
work. Through this work in various countries, I meet all sorts of chefs and use ingredients which influence
my cooking. This book is full of my Italian influences, and the three things that are close to my heart
where food is concerned: the essence of speed in preparation, a clean modern approach and the
importance of fresh ingredients. I would also like to thank Nicky Hill at Reed who gave me the opportunity
to write this book, which has been a challenge and a pleasure; my partner David Tatton who has been my
taster and tester with his hungry but critical palate; and David Loftus who took the photos, which I am
sure you will agree capture my three rules of cooking. Thank you everyone.

fran warde